THE SPIRIT OF ELIJAH

STUDY MANUAL

EXPOSE THE TRUTH.
EMBRACE GOD'S POWER.
BREAK THE ANTICHRIST SPIRIT.

Harrison House Books by Joseph Z

Demystifying the Prophetic: Understanding the Voice of God for the Coming Days of Fire

Servants of Fire: Secrets of the Unseen War & Angels Fighting for You

Breaking Hell's Economy: Your Guide to Last-Days Supernatural Provision

Breaking Hell's Economy Study Manual

Jesus and the Kingmakers

The Origin of the Cosmic Battle

The Spirit of Elijah

The Spirit of Elijah: Expose the Truth. Embrace God's Power. Break the Antichrist Spirit.

The Secret to the Life of John: A Revelation for a Supernaturally Long-Lasting Life

Weaponizing Your Faith

THE SPIRIT OF ELIJAH

STUDY MANUAL

EXPOSE THE TRUTH.
EMBRACE GOD'S POWER.
BREAK THE ANTICHRIST SPIRIT.

JOSEPH Z

All emphasis within Scripture quotations is the author's own.

Published by Harrison House Publishers
Shippensburg, PA 17257

ISBN 13 TP: 978-1-6675-1124-5
ISBN 13 eBook: 978-1-6675-1125-2

For Worldwide Distribution, Printed in the U.S.A.
1 2 3 4 5 6 7 8 / 29 28 27 26 25

CONTENTS

LETTER FROM JOSEPH

Understanding *The Spirit of Elijah* is a project drafted and architected directly from Scripture. For projects like this one, a solid biblical foundation is a must to avoid being lost in Christian lingo and spiritual pop culture without genuinely understanding the significance of the message. Preconceived notions and popularized ideas are put into proper order with the insertion of clear biblical representation, which leads to the effective meaning of this topic.

In the case of *The Spirit of Elijah*, it was of the highest importance to me that you, the reader, would be able to grasp and clearly understand this important message.

Darkness sows iniquity without repentance until an answer from God is given or reaped. Enter a reformer or one who similarly carries the spirit of Elijah to John the Baptist with a calling, message, and mandate to shake the institutions that once possessed a powerful and living revelation from God. These disrupters and change agents are activated in each generation, where darkness has sown and sown again without reprieve. Such was the case of Jezebel and Ahab, a demonic combination that is still impacting the lives of good believers today by labeled type and shadow but even more through demonic activity, which works its way into the Church, government, and marketplace.

The same Holy Spirit unction that moved Elijah to action and confrontation is readily available to work through the modern-day Church of Jesus. If you have received Jesus, you are part of that solution to generational assaults by evil.

One of the chapters of interest is where we take an in-depth look at the sons of Issachar. The parallels between what they did and what we are to do today should prove insightful and offer clarity for navigating your generation with discernment and prophetic understanding.

The Spirit of Elijah rises to expose the truth, embrace God's power, and counter the spirit of Antichrist.

I desire that this manual empowers and inspires you to know how to stand and what is available to those who rise in faith when darkness attempts to hijack a generation.

For Jesus,
Joseph Z

STUDY MANUAL INSTRUCTIONS

The Spirit of Elijah Study Manual was created to help individuals who want to deepen their understanding while reading *The Spirit of Elijah*. This manual is a companion to reading the book, with each section featuring questions and additional information for reflection. The answers are in the section you read in the book, but there's room for you to write your thoughts and answers. The "focus points" and "personal reflections" sections are opportunities for you to delve deeper and seek the Lord for answers, fostering personal growth. Some questions may require your honesty, and in moments of uncertainty, let the Holy Spirit help you.

God bless you in your journey in *The Spirit of Elijah*.

CHAPTER ONE

ONE REFORMER VERSUS AN ARMY OF DARKNESS

SCRIPTURES

1. First Kings 18:19 KJV—*Now therefore send, and gather to me all Israel unto mount Carmel, and the prophets of Baal four hundred and fifty, and the prophets of the groves four hundred, which eat at Jezebel's table.*

2. Judges 16:30—*Then Samson said, "Let me die with the Philistines!" And he pushed with all his might, and the temple fell on the lords and all the people who were in it. So the dead that he killed at his death were more than he had killed in his life.*

3. First Kings 18:20 KJV—*So Ahab sent unto all the children of Israel, and gathered the prophets together unto mount Carmel.*

4. First Kings 18:21-22 KJV—*And Elijah came unto all the people, and said, How long halt ye between two opinions? If the LORD be God, follow him: but if Baal, then follow him. And the people answered him not a word. 22 Then said Elijah unto the people, I, even I only, remain a prophet of the LORD; but Baal's prophets are four hundred and fifty men.*

5. Proverbs 29:2—*When the righteous are in authority, the people rejoice; but when a wicked man rules, the people groan.*

6. First Kings 18:24—*"Then you call on the name of your gods, and I will call on the name of the LORD; and the God who answers by fire, He is God." So all the people answered and said, "It is well spoken."*

7. First Corinthians 4:19-20—*But I will come to you shortly, if the Lord wills, and I will know, not the word of those who are puffed up, but the power. 20* ***For the kingdom of God is not in word but in power.***

8. First Thessalonians 1:5—*For our gospel did not come to you in word only, but also* ***in power****, and in the Holy Spirit and in much assurance, as you know what kind of men we were among you for your sake.*

9. First Corinthians 2:4—*And my speech and my preaching were not with persuasive words of human wisdom, but in* ***demonstration of the Spirit and of power.***

10. First Kings 18:22-26—*Then Elijah said to the people, "I alone am left a prophet of the LORD; but Baal's prophets are four hundred and fifty men. 23 Therefore let them give us two bulls; and let them choose one bull for themselves, cut it in pieces, and lay it on the wood, but put no fire under it; and I will prepare the other bull, and lay it on the wood, but put no fire under it. 24 Then you call on the name of your gods, and I will call on the name of the LORD; and the God who answers by fire, He is God." So all the people answered and said, "It is well spoken." 25 Now Elijah said to the prophets of Baal, "Choose one bull for yourselves and prepare it first, for you are many; and call on the name of your god, but put no fire under it." 26 So they took the bull which was given them, and they prepared it, and called on the name of Baal from morning even till noon, saying, "O Baal, hear us!" But there was no voice; no one answered. Then they leaped about the altar which they had made.*

11. First Kings 18:27-29—*And so it was, at noon, that Elijah mocked them and said, "Cry aloud, for he is a god; either he is meditating, or he is busy, or he is on a journey, or perhaps he is sleeping and must be awakened." 28 So they cried aloud, and cut themselves, as was their custom, with knives and lances, until the blood gushed out on them. 29 And when midday was past, they prophesied until the time of the offering of the evening sacrifice. But there was no voice; no one answered, no one paid attention.*

12. First Kings 18:30-36—*Then Elijah said to all the people, "Come near to me." So all the people came near to him. And he repaired the altar of the LORD that was broken down. 31 And Elijah took twelve stones, according to the number of the tribes of the sons of Jacob, to whom the word of the LORD had come, saying, "Israel shall be your name." 32 Then with the stones he built an altar in the name of the LORD; and he made a trench around the altar large enough to hold two seahs of seed. 33 And he put the wood in order, cut the bull in pieces, and laid it on the wood, and said, "Fill four waterpots with water, and pour it on the burnt sacrifice and on the wood." 34 Then he said, "Do it a second time," and they did it a second time; and he said, "Do it a third time," and they did it a third time. 35 So the water ran all around the altar; and he also filled the trench with water. 36 And it came to pass, at the time of the offering of the evening sacrifice, that Elijah the prophet came near and said, "LORD God of Abraham, Isaac, and Israel, let it be known this day that You are God in Israel and I am Your servant, and that I have done all these things at Your word."*

13. Isaiah 58:12 KJV—*And they that shall be of thee shall build the old waste places: thou shalt raise up the foundations of many generations; and thou shalt be called, The repairer of the breach, The restorer of paths to dwell in.*

14. First Kings 18:37-39— *"Hear me, O LORD, hear me, that this people may know that You are the LORD God, and that You have turned their hearts back to You again." 38 Then the fire of the LORD fell and consumed the burnt sacrifice, and the wood and the stones and the dust, and it licked up the water that was in the trench. 39 Now when all the people saw it, they fell on their faces; and they said, "The LORD, He is God! The LORD, He is God!"*

15. First Kings 18:40—*And Elijah said to them, "Seize the prophets of Baal! Do not let one of them escape!" So they seized them; and Elijah brought them down to the Brook Kishon and executed them there.*

16. First Kings 18:41-46—*Then Elijah said to Ahab, "Go up, eat and drink; for there is the sound of abundance of rain." 42 So Ahab went up to eat and drink. And Elijah went up to the top of Carmel; then he bowed down on the ground, and put his face between his knees, 43 and said to his servant, "Go up now, look toward the sea." So he went up and looked, and said, "There is nothing." And seven times he said, "Go again." 44 Then it came to pass the seventh time, that he said, "There is a cloud, as small as a man's hand, rising out of the sea!" So he said, "Go up, say to Ahab,*

'Prepare your chariot, and go down before the rain stops you.'" 45 Now it happened in the meantime that the sky became black with clouds and wind, and there was a heavy rain. So Ahab rode away and went to Jezreel. 46 Then the hand of the LORD came upon Elijah; and he girded up his loins and ran ahead of Ahab to the entrance of Jezreel.

We see in 1 Kings that the nation of Israel was amid a horrible famine. The people were so desperate for rain that they appeared at Mount Carmel when summoned. Why do you think the Lord uses circumstances, such as a drought in the land, to rightsize a nation?

____

____

____

____

____

____

____

____

____

____

____

____

____

AHAB THOUGHT THE ADVANTAGE WAS HIS

King Ahab rode the fence of indecisiveness. He wouldn't choose between Baal or the One True God. He wanted both. In this situation, deciding to meet Elijah on Mount Carmel had Ahab leaning more toward the side of Baal. He thought the prophets of this vile religion had the advantage. Under divine order, the prophet of God was given a strategic location to face Jezebel's demonic horde. Why do you think God chose this particular location, and what were the implications to Ahab?

A MAN WITH A REVELATION IS NOT AT THE MERCY OF A CULTURE GONE MAD

We often feel isolated, like Elijah, who thought he was the sole prophet. The devil is adept at this, filling our minds with falsehoods. Elijah came alone to stand up to 850 ungodly characters. He could do this because he had a revelation from God! Reflect on a time when God gave you a revelation that seemed impossible to accomplish on your own. What was that time, and how did God help you bring it to pass?

REFORMERS OFFER THE CULTURE A CHOICE

Just like King Ahab was on the fence of indecisiveness, the people were also riding the fence. Which is why Elijah asked them, "How long will you falter between two opinions?" We see people who were unsure whom to worship. Why? Could it be because they had a king who wouldn't choose, or they had been oppressed for so long under a wicked culture? Fear could have swayed their choice. Notice that the people did not say a word in response to Elijah's question. Why do you think they were silent?

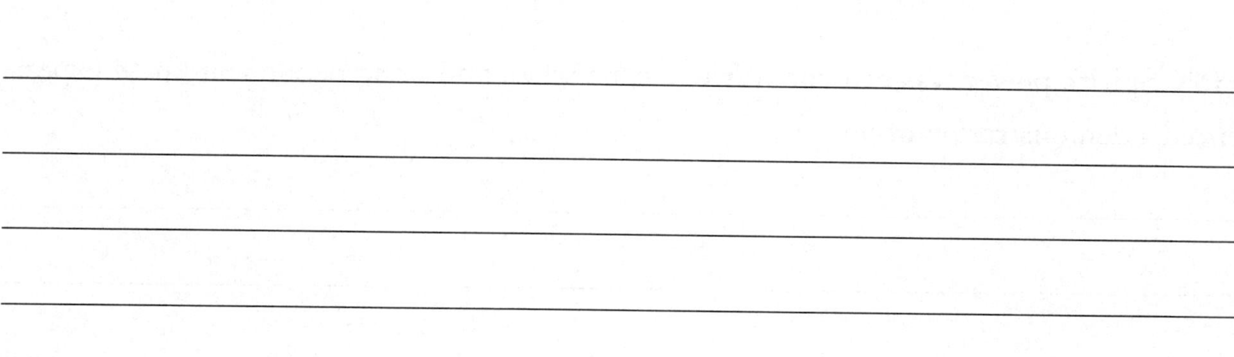

ELIJAH OFFERED THEM A DEMONSTRATION—THE GOD WHO ANSWERS BY FIRE!

FOCUS POINT

"Then you call on the name of your gods, and I will call on the name of the LORD; and the God who answers by fire, He is God." So all the people answered and said, "It is well spoken."

—1 Kings 18:24

We are living in a "show me" culture. There are reasons why social media is exploding: people want to see more. Show us more fun and excitement, examples, how-tos, etc. Similar to the culture of Elijah's time, the people wanted to see something to help them believe. If a generation of people will be won over to Jesus, they need willing believers who will take the step of faith, just like Elijah, and show them who the One True Living God is. We are surrounded by the lost and dying world that needs an encounter with Jesus to change their lives for eternity. Take this time to pray for your lost loved ones and ask the Lord to show you ways to minister to them so they will hear and respond.

REMEMBER THE WORDS OF THE APOSTLE PAUL

In 1 Corinthians 4:19-20, 1 Thessalonians 1:5, and 1 Corinthians 2:4, the gospel is delivered in word and power. These acts of power can range from a healing, a financial breakthrough, or a once hard-hearted person encountering Jesus. Whatever the scenario, the

Holy Spirit's power was evident. Write a time when you or someone you know experienced a demonstration of power.

ELIJAH SET UP THE RULES OF ENGAGEMENT

"A man or woman with a word from God is not at the mercy of a culture going mad." Sadly, many people will have a word from the Lord and silence it because they don't feel comfortable releasing this word. For some, being politically correct is more important than what God instructs them to do. Many in the Church are silent. It's time for us to be bold and rise with our God-given word and release it. What needs to happen for this to become a reality? What is your role or commitment to help bring about change?

REFORMERS SPEAK OUT SOMETIMES WITH SARCASM AGAINST EVIL!

In 1 Kings 18:27-29, the prophets of Baal were crying aloud and cutting themselves. Elijah teased them and encouraged them to cry louder. Maybe their god was sleeping or on vacation. Why do you think so many follow other gods when they don't see evidence of that god being real?

REFORMERS REPAIR HOLY RUINS

The enemy is trying to destroy believers and keep them from giving the Lord their lives and sacrificing their "flesh" (sinful tendencies and the power within that leads to sin) at the foot of the Cross. Similar to 1 Kings 18:30, where the altar was broken down and Elijah repaired it, we are to repair the "altar" by renewing our minds daily according to the Word of God. How can you resist the enemy's destructive ways and protect the "altar" of your heart toward God?

REFORMERS USHER IN THE FIRE OF GOD

By demonstration, the Lord revealed Himself to the people, and according to 1 Kings 18:37, the Lord "turned their hearts back to Him again." God desires the lost to turn their hearts to Him and find Him. What are ways that God does this?

REFORMERS EXECUTE JUDGMENT OF EVIL

In 1 Kings 18:40, Elijah executed the prophets of Baal. Justice was served against the agents of idolatry. According to Ephesians 6:12, "For we do not wrestle against flesh and blood, but against principalities, against powers, against the rulers of the darkness of this age, against spiritual hosts of wickedness in the heavenly places." We are in a war against the devil and his wicked demonic hordes. Thankfully, we have Jesus on our side to help us fight this battle, and He will bring justice to Satan and his followers in the end.

REFORMERS BRING THE RAIN

Reformers usher in a blessing. However, one must remove the obstacle blocking the Lord's blessing to accomplish this. In the case of Elijah, he had to confront the 850 prophets and bring judgment on them. Once this was done, the rain came!

In Matthew 17:20, Jesus says, "I say to you, if you have faith as a mustard seed, you will say to this mountain, 'Move from here to there,' and it will move; and nothing will be impossible for you." When Elijah's servant saw the cloud, which was as small as a man's hand, Elijah's faith knew that rain was coming. Have you been in a place where you believed for the Lord's blessing in an area, but something was blocking your breakthrough? What steps did you take to confront, apply your faith, and receive your breakthrough blessing?

____

____

____

____

____

____

____

____

____

WE MUST PARTICIPATE

PERSONAL REFLECTIONS

God has called His Body to reach the lost; you are an integral part of this plan. We see this in Matthew 28:19, where Jesus says, "Go therefore and make disciples of all nations, baptizing them in the name of the Father and of the Son and of the Holy Spirit." Going into the world is anywhere outside of your home. We need to be willing vessels who see a need and fill it. The current worldwide need is a lost and dying world on its way to crisis eternity, and your role in addressing this need is invaluable.

How did the "The Impact of One" section help and encourage you to be a voice, even if it's to one person, knowing that through that "one," you could reach thousands, if not millions, for Jesus?

CHAPTER TWO

THE WITCH AND HER UNSCRUPULOUS KING

SCRIPTURES

1. First Kings 16:29-34—*In the thirty-eighth year of Asa king of Judah, Ahab the son of Omri became king over Israel; and Ahab the son of Omri reigned over Israel in Samaria twenty-two years. 30 Now Ahab the son of Omri did evil in the sight of the LORD, more than all who were before him. 31 And it came to pass, as though it had been a trivial thing for him to walk in the sins of Jeroboam the son of Nebat, that he took as wife Jezebel the daughter of Ethbaal, king of the Sidonians; and he went and served Baal and worshiped him. 32 Then he set up an altar for Baal in the temple of Baal, which he had built in Samaria. 33 And Ahab made a wooden image. Ahab did more to provoke the LORD God of Israel to anger than all the kings of Israel who were before him. 34 In his days Hiel of Bethel built Jericho. He laid its foundation with Abiram his firstborn, and with his youngest son Segub he set up its gates, according to the word of the LORD, which He had spoken through Joshua the son of Nun.*

2. Second Kings 9:22—*Now it happened, when Joram saw Jehu, that he said, "Is it peace, Jehu?" So he answered, "What peace, as long as the harlotries of your mother Jezebel and her witchcraft are so many?"*

3. *Proverbs 25:26*—*A righteous man who falters before the wicked is like a murky spring and a polluted well.*

4. *First Kings 18:21*—*And Elijah came to all the people, and said, "How long will you falter between two opinions? If the LORD is God, follow Him; but if Baal, follow him."*

5. *Revelation 2:20*—*Nevertheless I have a few things against you, because you allow that woman Jezebel, who calls herself a prophetess, to teach and seduce My servants to commit sexual immorality and eat things sacrificed to idols.*

6. *James 3:1*—*My brethren, let not many of you become teachers, knowing that we shall receive a stricter judgment.*

7. *Matthew 24:11*—*Then many false prophets will rise up and deceive many.*

8. *Revelation 2:14*—*But I have a few things against you, because you have there those who hold the doctrine of Balaam, who taught Balak to put a stumbling block before the children of Israel, to eat things sacrificed to idols, and to commit sexual immorality.*

9. *Revelation 2:6*—*But this you have, that you hate the deeds of the Nicolaitans, which I also hate.*

10. *Revelation 2:15*—*Thus you also have those who hold the doctrine of the Nicolaitans, which thing I hate.*

11. *Acts 6:5*—*And the saying pleased the whole multitude. And they chose Stephen, a man full of faith and the Holy Spirit, and Philip, Prochorus, Nicanor, Timon, Parmenas, and Nicolas, a proselyte from Antioch.*

12. *First Corinthians 10:25-31*—*Eat whatever is sold in the meat market, asking no questions for conscience' sake; 26 for "the earth is the Lord's, and all its fullness." 27 If any of those who do not believe invites you to dinner, and you desire to go, eat whatever is set before you, asking no question for conscience' sake. 28 But if anyone says to you, "This was offered to idols," do not eat it for the sake of the one who told you, and for conscience' sake; for "the earth is the Lord's, and all its fullness." 29 "Conscience," I say, not your own, but that of the other. For why is my liberty judged by another man's* *conscience? 30 But if I partake with thanks, why am I evil spoken of for the food over which I give thanks? 31 Therefore, whether you eat or drink, or whatever you do, do all to the glory of God.*

13. First John 3:19-21—*And by this we know that we are of the truth, and shall assure our hearts before Him. 20 For if our heart condemns us, God is greater than our heart, and knows all things. 21 Beloved, if our heart does not condemn us, we have confidence toward God.*

14. Hebrews 10:22—*Let us draw near with a true heart in full assurance of faith, having our hearts sprinkled from an evil conscience and our bodies washed with pure water.*

15. First Kings 19:2—*Then Jezebel sent a messenger to Elijah, saying, "So let the gods do to me, and more also, if I do not make your life as the life of one of them by tomorrow about this time."*

16. Revelation 11:15—*Then the seventh angel sounded: And there were loud voices in heaven, saying, "The kingdoms of this world have become the kingdoms of our Lord and His Christ, and He shall reign forever and ever!"*

What behaviors did Jezebel have that would suggest she was demonically possessed?

____

____

____

____

____

____

____

____

____

____

FATHER AND MOTHER OF EVIL

Ahab and Jezebel were a counterfeit father and mother to a nation. The devil will always copy God's original plans. Satan is not a creator, so he will duplicate what he sees. The only thing is, he perverts and corrupts things. In this instance, he used Ahab and Jezebel to represent parental roles but in a vile manner. List some character traits of a counterfeit mother and father versus legitimate parents.

AHAB WAS THE WORST OF THIS WICKED DUO

Why was Ahab considered the worst kind of leader when compared to Jezebel, a monster of a human being?

AHAB, AN UNSCRUPULOUS KING

FOCUS POINT

When someone is all about "self," they will look past certain things, even if they are evil, if it benefits them personally. How can we avoid this type of person or prevent ourselves from becoming one?

THE SPIRIT OF AHAB

What descriptions of the spirit of Ahab surprised you or brought revelation to your understanding of this particular spirit or demon?

JEZEBEL INFLUENCED THE NATION

List several ways that Jezebel influenced the nation.

THAT WOMAN JEZEBEL IN THYATIRA

According to Revelation 2:20, "that woman" refers to the pastor's wife in the church of Thyatira. What did this woman do to receive the title "Jezebel"?

JEZEBEL CALLED HERSELF A PRIESTESS

Why does the spirit of Jezebel often disguise itself as a prophet?

JEZEBEL TAUGHT IN THE CHURCH

Surprisingly, many Jezebels are in the Church today. Why do you think these types can get into these positions?

JEZEBEL SEDUCED THE PEOPLE OF GOD

When looking at the definition of "seduce," *to distract or take someone off their assignment*, how has this changed your previous understanding of the word? Knowing this, how can you identify the spirit of Jezebel at work in the Church?

JEZEBEL OFFERED THEM AN AVENUE OR ENCOURAGEMENT TO SEXUAL IMMORALITY

Unfortunately, we see Jezebel at work in the Church pushing the agenda of sexual immorality. Some pastors say that certain sexual sins are not sins. They do this to push an agenda and justify their stance. Why do you think so many are encouraging these things when the Bible talks against all forms of sexual sin and perversion?

FALSE PROPHETS HAVE SIMILAR DOCTRINE

A common characteristic of false prophets is that they pervert grace and encourage behavior that opposes the Scriptures. This is why discernment is vital among believers, so these types will not be allowed behind pulpits.

JEZEBEL LIKEWISE ENCOURAGED OR OFFERED A PATH TO EATING THINGS SACRIFICED TO IDOLS

Abstaining from eating things sacrificed to idols was not only for believers but also those new to the Church. List other things Christians should avoid so new Christians don't become confused or have their consciences hurt.

JEZEBEL WAS ALLOWED—SHE HAD PERMISSION

Why are those who consent to the vile behavior of others just as guilty as the one doing the very act? Why is their silence contributing to the evil force working through an individual?

THE ISSUE OF A GUILTY CONSCIENCE IS A MECHANISM USED BY JEZEBEL AND FALSE PROPHETS

God is the same yesterday, today, and forever. He never changes. He has loved His creation from the beginning, which is why Jesus was sent to save the lost. Jesus did not come to condemn the world but to save it (see John 3:17). When we understand this, we can have confidence in God and understand that if God doesn't condemn us, we don't have to either.

CHARACTERISTICS OF A JEZEBEL SPIRIT

What characteristics of a Jezebel spirit stood out to you and gave you a new understanding of how this spirit operates?

THE JEZEBEL DEMON STILL OPPOSES ELIJAH TODAY

The Jezebel spirit is still intimidating legitimate prophets today. Sadly, many are in hiding because of the threats presented by those walking under the influence of the vile spirit. We need these prophets to stand up like Elijah and say, "No more! We will not back down!" What steps can be taken to "not back down" and stand in confidence and authority against a Jezebel spirit?

VILE BAAL WORSHIP WAS INTRODUCED AND ELEVATED IN THE NATION

Write a brief description of who and what Baal was.

CHILD SACRIFICE AND TRANSSEXUALITY WERE PART OF WORSHIP

The culture during Jezebel's time was so vile that it said a child was similar to a calf, and they justified the murder of so many innocent children. Today, we see this happening in clinics all around the world. Babies are said to be only fetuses while in a mother's womb. Society has dehumanized the innocent and has made abortion acceptable. We need to be a voice for those who don't have a voice and stand for what is right.

AHAB REBUILDS THE CURSED CITY!

Ahab was not only wicked but also dense and rebellious, avoiding Joshua's words that Jericho should not be rebuilt. When evil is accepted and allowed to flourish, truth and obedience will be nonexistent.

THE ONLY ANSWER TO DARKNESS IS LIGHT!

Darkness is all around. While believers are still on earth, we are to be a light to those around us. How should Christians show the light and expose the darkness?

EVEN ON A BAD DAY, YOU ARE ANOINTED TO BE THE BEST THERE IS!

When you feel you aren't qualified or that God can't use you, remember that He desires to use anyone who answers the call and says, "Yes, Lord, I am here. Use me." It doesn't matter whether you are qualified or not. What matters is that you say, "Yes." What is God calling you to say "yes" to?

HOW TO RESIST JEZEBEL

PERSONAL REFLECTIONS

The spirit of Jezebel has shown its ugly face throughout history in many ways. We see that the spirit of Jezebel and Ahab work hand in hand. We must be filled with the Holy Spirit and walk in wisdom and discernment to identify these vile spirits and cast them out. Take this time to ask the Holy Spirit to speak to you, help you be aware of these types of spirits, and equip you to cast them out. Write your prayer down.

CHAPTER THREE

A GENERATION AT WAR WITH GOD

SCRIPTURES

1. Romans 1:21-25—*Because, although they knew God, they did not glorify Him as God, nor were thankful, but became futile in their thoughts, and their foolish hearts were darkened. 22 Professing to be wise, they became fools, 23 and changed the glory of the incorruptible God into an image made like corruptible man—and birds and four-footed animals and creeping things. 24 Therefore God also gave them up to uncleanness, in the lusts of their hearts, to dishonor their bodies among themselves, 25 who exchanged the truth of God for the lie, and worshiped and served the creature rather than the Creator, who is blessed forever. Amen.*

2. Jonah 2:8—*Those who regard worthless idols forsake their own Mercy.*

3. Jonah 4:2—*So he prayed to the LORD, and said, "Ah, LORD, was not this what I said when I was still in my country? Therefore I fled previously to Tarshish; for I know that You are a gracious and merciful God, slow to anger and abundant in lovingkindness, One who relents from doing harm."*

4. Luke 1:17—*He will also go before Him* ***in the spirit and power of Elijah,*** *"to turn the hearts of the fathers to the children," and the disobedient to the wisdom of the just, to make ready a people prepared for the Lord.*

5. *First John 2:18-27*—*Little children, it is the last hour; and as you have heard that the **Antichrist is coming,** even now **many antichrists have come,** by which we know that it is the last hour. 19 They went out from us, but they were not of us; for if they had been of us, they would have continued with us; but they went out that they might be made manifest, that none of them were of us. 20 But you have an anointing from the Holy One, and you know all things. 21 I have not written to you because you do not know the truth, but because you know it, and that no lie is of the truth. 22 Who is a liar but he who denies that Jesus is the Christ? He is antichrist who denies the Father and the Son. 23 Whoever denies the Son does not have the Father either; he who acknowledges the Son has the Father also. 24 Therefore let that abide in you which you heard from the beginning. If what you heard from the beginning abides in you, you also will abide in the Son and in the Father. 25 And this is the promise that He has promised us—eternal life. 26 These things I have written to you concerning those who try to deceive you. 27 But the anointing which you have received from Him abides in you, and you do not need that anyone teach you; but as the same anointing teaches you concerning all things, and is true, and is not a lie, and just as it has taught you, you will abide in Him.*

6. *Second Thessalonians 2:3*—*Let no one deceive you by any means; for that Day will not come unless the falling away comes first, and the man of sin is revealed, the son of perdition.*

7. *Matthew 24:3-8*—*Now as He sat on the Mount of Olives, the disciples came to Him privately, saying, "Tell us, when will these things be? And what will be the sign of Your coming, and of the end of the age?" 4 And Jesus answered and said to them: "Take heed that no one deceives you. 5 For many will come in My name, saying, 'I am the Christ,' and will deceive many. 6 And you will hear of wars and rumors of wars. See that you are not troubled; for all these things must come to pass, but the end is not yet. 7 For nation will rise against nation, and kingdom against kingdom. And there will be famines, pestilences, and earthquakes in various places. 8 All these are the beginning of sorrows."*

8. *Ezekiel 28:14*—*You were the anointed cherub who covers; I established you; you were on the holy mountain of God; you walked back and forth in the midst of fiery stones.*

9. Exodus 3:1—*Now Moses was tending the flock of Jethro his father-in-law, the priest of Midian. And he led the flock to the back of the desert, and came to Horeb, the* ***mountain of God.***

10. Exodus 4:27—*And the Lord said to Aaron, "Go into the wilderness to meet Moses." So he went and met him on the* ***mountain of God****, and kissed him.*

11. Exodus 18:5—*And Jethro, Moses' father-in-law, came with his sons and his wife to Moses in the wilderness, where he was encamped at the* ***mountain of God.***

12. Exodus 24:13—*So Moses arose with his assistant Joshua, and Moses went up to the* ***mountain of God.***

13. First Kings 19:8—*So he arose, and ate and drank; and he went in the strength of that food forty days and forty nights as far as Horeb, the* ***mountain of God.***

14. Matthew 4:5-9—*Then the devil took Him up into the holy city, set Him on the pinnacle of the temple, 6 and said to Him, "If You are the Son of God, throw Yourself down. For it is written: 'He shall give His angels charge over you,' and, 'In their hands they shall bear you up, lest you dash your foot against a stone.'" 7 Jesus said to him, "It is written again, 'You shall not tempt the LORD your God.'" 8 Again, the devil took Him up on an exceedingly high mountain, and showed Him all the kingdoms of the world and their glory. 9 And he said to Him, "All these things I will give You if You will fall down and worship me."*

15. Luke 4:5-7—*Then the devil, taking Him up on a high mountain, showed Him all the kingdoms of the world in a moment of time. 6 And the devil said to Him, "All this authority I will give You, and their glory; for this has been delivered to me, and I give it to whomever I wish. 7 Therefore, if You will worship before me, all will be Yours."*

16. John 12:31-33—*"Now is the judgment of this world; now the ruler of this world will be cast out. 32 And I, if I am lifted up from the earth, will draw all peoples to Myself." 33 This He said, signifying by what death He would die.*

17. Matthew 28:18—*And Jesus came and spoke to them, saying, "All authority has been given to Me in heaven and on earth."*

18. First John 4:17—*Love has been perfected among us in this: that we may have boldness in the day of judgment; because as He is, so are we in this world.*

19. Ephesians 6:12—*For we do not wrestle against flesh and blood, but against principalities, against powers, against the rulers of the darkness of this age, against spiritual hosts of wickedness in the heavenly places.*

According to Romans 1:21-25, when someone is not glorifying God or being thankful, this can lead to foolishness and eventually bring rebellion in the heart and mind toward God. Why do you think giving God glory and having a grateful heart is so important?

List some reasons why you think Jonah was upset that Nineveh was saved from destruction. Have you ever felt this way toward a person or group? If so, what helped you offer forgiveness to them?

THE SPIRIT OF ANTICHRIST AND THE WAR FOR RECONCILIATION

In every generation, the god of this world (Satan) has willing vessels ready to be used to do horrendous acts against the children of the One True God. This is why Elijah is coming to declare war on the spirit of the age. We need to be willing vessels to be used by God to win the battle of light versus darkness.

DEFINING THE SPIRIT OF ANTICHRIST

Write a brief description of what the spirit of Antichrist is and what it thrives on.

WE ARE FACING THE SPIRIT OF ANTICHRIST IN OUR CULTURE

With what you have learned concerning the spirit of Antichrist, list some figures throughout history who could have been mistaken as the Antichrist but today are identified as walking in the spirit of Antichrist. An example would be Hitler.

WAR OF REFORMATION AGAINST THE SPIRIT OF ANTICHRIST

In the previous question, you listed several people throughout history who could have acted in the spirit of Antichrist. Keeping those names in mind, list those God used as His agents and who went into the battle zone against these characters the devil used.

DE-THRONING SATAN'S TERRITORY

FOCUS POINT

In Matthew 4:5-9 and Luke 4:5-7, the devil tempts Jesus in several ways. Jesus' response was, "It is written...." Jesus knew the Word, understood it, and used His authority to stand against the temptations. Because of this, the devil left Jesus alone. These three steps are vital for every believer. Knowing the Word, understanding it, and using our God-given authority to stand when the enemy wants us to give into temptation. Take this time to get in the Word. Ask the Lord to speak to you as you read and meditate on what you read. It's good to memorize scriptures so when the enemy comes, you can say, "It is written... now leave me alone."

JESUS SEIZED THE DEVIL'S TERRITORY

It is interesting to think that Satan honestly thought he would be able to tempt Jesus and persuade Him to do what he said. Satan thought it would be easy, like it was with Adam. Throughout each decade, the devil has had many people say yes to him. This could be why he was gullible in thinking that Jesus would respond the same way. Thankfully, Jesus didn't! Just like Jesus overcame the enemy and his temptations, we can do the same! (See John 16:33.)

HOW IS THE DEVIL STILL HERE IF JESUS WON?

Jesus won victory over the devil when He rose from the dead, yet the devil still influences non-believers on earth. What steps should believers take to resist the enemy and combat his schemes against humanity?

____

____

____

ANCIENT DEMONS MUST BE DRIVEN OUT!

PERSONAL REFLECTIONS

The spirit of Antichrist is a destructive spirit that seeks to destroy the people of God. Through Jesus, this spirit can be pushed back and stopped. The body of Christ is equipped to stand against this vile demon and win every battle. Until Jesus returns, we are here to be a light against the darkness. Read Ephesians 6:10-20, and write these verses. We must be ready in and out of season, equipped with our armor, and positioned to stand when the enemy attacks.

CHAPTER FOUR

WHERE DARKNESS REIGNS, *A REFORMER WILL RISE*

SCRIPTURES

1. First Kings 17:1-7—*And Elijah the Tishbite, of the inhabitants of Gilead, said to Ahab, "As the LORD God of Israel lives, before whom I stand, there shall not be dew nor rain these years, except at my word." 2 Then the word of the LORD came to him, saying, 3 "Get away from here and turn eastward, and hide by the Brook Cherith, which flows into the Jordan. 4 And it will be that you shall drink from the brook, and I have commanded the ravens to feed you there." 5 So he went and did according to the word of the LORD, for he went and stayed by the Brook Cherith, which flows into the Jordan. 6 The ravens brought him bread and meat in the morning, and bread and meat in the evening; and he drank from the brook. 7 And it happened after a while that the brook dried up, because there had been no rain in the land.*

2. First Kings 18:1—*And it came to pass after many days that the word of the LORD came to Elijah, in the third year, saying, "Go, present yourself to Ahab, and I will send rain on the earth."*

3. First Kings 18:17-18—*Then it happened, when Ahab saw Elijah, that Ahab said to him, "Is that you, O troubler of Israel?" 18 And he answered, "I have not troubled Israel, but you and your father's house have, in that you have forsaken the commandments of the LORD and have followed the Baals."*

4. First Kings 21:1-16—*And it came to pass after these things that Naboth the Jezreelite had a vineyard which was in Jezreel, next to the palace of Ahab king of Samaria. 2 So Ahab spoke to Naboth, saying, "Give me your vineyard, that I may have it for a vegetable garden, because it is near, next to my house; and for it I will give you a vineyard better than it. Or, if it seems good to you, I will give you its worth in money." 3 But Naboth said to Ahab, "The LORD forbid that I should give the inheritance of my fathers to you!" 4 So Ahab went into his house sullen and displeased because of the word which Naboth the Jezreelite had spoken to him; for he had said, "I will not give you the inheritance of my fathers." And he lay down on his bed, and turned away his face, and would eat no food. 5 But Jezebel his wife came to him, and said to him, "Why is your spirit so sullen that you eat no food?" 6 He said to her, "Because I spoke to Naboth the Jezreelite, and said to him, 'Give me your vineyard for money; or else, if it pleases you, I will give you another vineyard for it.' And he answered, 'I will not give you my vineyard.'" 7 Then Jezebel his wife said to him, "You now exercise authority over Israel! Arise, eat food, and let your heart be cheerful; I will give you the vineyard of Naboth the Jezreelite." 8 And she wrote letters in Ahab's name, sealed them with his seal, and sent the letters to the elders and the nobles who were dwelling in the city with Naboth. 9 She wrote in the letters, saying, Proclaim a fast, and seat Naboth with high honor among the people; 10 and seat two men, scoundrels, before him to bear witness against him, saying, "You have blasphemed God and the king." Then take him out, and stone him, that he may die. 11 So the men of his city, the elders and nobles who were inhabitants of his city, did as Jezebel had sent to them, as it was written in the letters which she had sent to them. 12 They proclaimed a fast, and seated Naboth with high honor among the people. 13 And two men, scoundrels, came in and sat before him; and the scoundrels witnessed against him, against Naboth, in the presence of the people, saying, "Naboth has blasphemed God and the king!" Then they took him outside the city and stoned him with stones, so that he died. 14 Then they sent to Jezebel, saying, "Naboth has been stoned and is dead." 15 And it came to pass, when Jezebel heard that Naboth had been stoned and was dead, that Jezebel said to Ahab, "Arise, take possession of the vineyard of Naboth the Jezreelite, which he refused to give you for money; for Naboth is not alive, but dead." 16 So it was, when Ahab heard that Naboth was dead, that Ahab got up and went down to take possession of the vineyard of Naboth the Jezreelite.*

5. Galatians 1:4—*Who gave Himself for our sins, that He might deliver us from this present evil age, according to the will of our God and Father.*

6. Ecclesiastes 1:10-11—*Is there anything of which it may be said, "See, this is new"? It has already been in ancient times before us. 11 There is no remembrance of former things, nor will there be any remembrance of things that are to come by those who will come after.*

7. Psalm 27:13—*I would have lost heart, unless I had believed that I would see the goodness of the Lord in the land of the living.*

8. Revelation 12:7-9—*And war broke out in heaven: Michael and his angels fought with the dragon; and the dragon and his angels fought, 8 but they did not prevail, nor was a place found for them in heaven any longer. 9 So the great dragon was cast out, that serpent of old, called the Devil and Satan, who deceives the whole world; he was cast to the earth, and his angels were cast out with him.*

9. Second Corinthians 4:3-4—*But even if our gospel is veiled, it is veiled to those who are perishing, 4 whose minds the god of this age has blinded, who do not believe, lest the light of the gospel of the glory of Christ, who is the image of God, should shine on them.*

10. Hebrews 11:7—*By faith Noah, being divinely warned of things not yet seen, moved with godly fear, prepared an ark for the saving of his household, by which he condemned the world and became heir of the righteousness which is according to faith.*

11. Second Peter 2:5—*And did not spare the ancient world, but saved Noah, one of eight people, a preacher of righteousness, bringing in the flood on the world of the ungodly.*

12. Proverbs 29:2—*When the righteous are in authority, the people rejoice; but when a wicked man rules, the people groan.*

13. Mark 3:1-6—*And He entered the synagogue again, and a man was there who had a withered hand. 2 So they watched Him closely, whether He would heal him on the Sabbath, so that they might accuse Him. 3 And He said to the man who had the withered hand, "Step forward." 4 Then He said to them, "Is it lawful on the Sabbath to do good or to do evil, to save life or to kill?" But they kept silent. 5 And* ***when He had looked around at them with anger, being grieved by the hardness of their hearts, He said to the man, "Stretch out your hand." And he stretched it out, and***

his hand was restored as whole as the other. *6 Then the Pharisees went out and immediately plotted with the Herodians against Him, how they might destroy Him.*

14. Malachi 3:12—*"And all nations will call you blessed, for you will be a delightful land," says the Lord of hosts.*

15. Proverbs 13:22—*A good man leaves an inheritance to his children's children, but the wealth of the sinner is stored up for the righteous.*

16. Isaiah 45:3—*I will give you the treasures of darkness and hidden riches of secret places, that you may know that I, the Lord, who call you by your name, Am the God of Israel.*

17. First Corinthians 1:21—*For since, in the wisdom of God, the world through wisdom did not know God, it pleased God through the foolishness of the message preached to save those who believe.*

18. Romans 10:14—*How then shall they call on Him in whom they have not believed? And how shall they believe in Him of whom they have not heard? And how shall they hear without a preacher?*

19. Jeremiah 4:3—*For thus says the LORD to the men of Judah and Jerusalem: "Break up your fallow ground, and do not sow among thorns."*

20. Hosea 10:12—*Sow for yourselves righteousness; reap in mercy; break up your fallow ground, for it is time to seek the LORD, till He comes and rains righteousness on you.*

21. Second Peter 3:11-12—*Therefore, since all these things will be dissolved, what manner of persons ought you to be in holy conduct and godliness, 12 looking for and hastening the coming of the day of God, because of which the heavens will be dissolved, being on fire, and the elements will melt with fervent heat?*

22. Joel 2:11—*...for the day of the LORD is great and very terrible; who can endure it?*

23. Revelation 6:17—*For the great day of His wrath has come, and who is able to stand?*

24. Psalm 149:6-9 NASB1995—*Let the high praises of God be in their mouth, and a two-edged sword in their hand, 7 to execute vengeance on the nations, and punishment on the peoples; 8 to bind their kings with chains, and their nobles with fetters of iron; 9 to execute on them the written judgment—This is an honor for all His godly ones. Praise the LORD!*

25. Second Corinthians 10:3-6 NASB1995—*For though we walk in the flesh, we do not war according to the flesh, 4 for the weapons of our warfare are not of the flesh, but divinely powerful for the destruction of fortresses. 5 We are destroying speculations and every lofty thing raised up against the knowledge of God, and we are taking every thought captive to the obedience of Christ, 6 and we are ready to punish all disobedience, whenever your obedience is complete.*

26. Psalm 126:5—*Those who sow in tears shall reap in joy.*

YOU CANNOT TWIST THE FABRIC OF REALITY

Throughout history, people have influenced society through their actions in every culture. What are some historical examples of these actions backfiring, whether for good or bad?

The act of sowing and reaping works for both good and evil. Whoever sows evil will reap evil. Jezebel and Ahab sowed the most vile and evil things; thankfully, God sent Elijah as a reformer to confront these wicked acts. Have you experienced the fruit of things you have sown, both good and bad? If so, what lesson did you learn through the harvest you reaped?

THE TIDE HAD TURNED

When people are under duress and hardships, anything can lead them to hear a reformer when liberty is presented. A severe drought brought Israel to a place where they were desperate for the turn of the tide. Do you believe we, as a nation, may be close to a tipping point? What might that point be? Why or why not?

WHEN PEOPLE LIVE FOR NOTHING, THEY WILL SERVE THE HIGHEST BIDDER

Please read 1 Kings 21:1-16. What did you learn about Jezebel and Ahab in the story of Naboth's vineyard?

ELIJAH CAME TO DESTROY THE WORKS OF EVIL

FOCUS POINT

Today, the spirit of Jezebel is present. We must be on the lookout for reformers to rise and reclaim a hijacked generation. In our day and age, do you see reformers working in the spirit of Elijah, standing up against the spirit of Jezebel? If so, list some of them here. Pray for supernatural protection over those you wrote down.

THERE IS NOTHING NEW UNDER THE SUN

Jesus is coming back for His bride soon. We are here for such a time as this to be a light against the darkness. As we see history repeat itself, we need to be people who have a foundation in the Word of God and are ready for whatever presents itself, good and bad. Remember that through all situations, we, as believers, are blessed. (See Matthew 5:3-16.) Knowing that you were born for such a time as this, what is God calling you to do to be a light shining in the darkness?

THE END OF THE AGE WAS INEVITABLE FROM THE ORIGINAL REBELLION

With everything happening worldwide, many are asleep and aren't concerned about the direction things are going. Why do you think this is an everyday reality for many believers?

BREAKING A MIND-BLINDING SPIRIT

Society is facing an agenda that wants to destroy and lead many away from the knowledge of God. This agenda was once hidden and done in secret but is now very evident. There is no more hiding; things are done in the open, and we are supposed to accept it to be "politically correct." What are ways that you see this today, and how should we, as believers, respond against these schemes and tactics of the enemy?

GOD'S SECRET WEAPON

You are God's secret weapon to stand against the wicked agendas of our time. Do you feel prepared for this role, or do you need to get your armor on and get ready for battle? What steps are you willing to take so that you are ready?

SPECIAL ANOINTING FOR YOUR GENERATION

Just like God used Noah to preach righteousness to a perverse generation, He is looking for willing vessels who will do the same today. In every culture, some walk in the path of righteousness, and some don't. God needs believers to not only be righteous but also minister to those who are dying and on their way to a crisis eternity in hell. Let's be willing to be used by the Lord in this way and bring God His lost creation so they can become His sons and daughters. What will you do with this knowledge?

SOME THINGS THAT HARDEN THE HEARTS OF A CULTURE

List the things that harden the hearts of a culture and why a display of power is crucial to counter this type of culture.

SIGNS OF A CULTURE SET FREE

List the signs that show a culture is set free. Are you seeing any of these signs in the culture today? Explain your answer.

PROPHETS AND REFORMERS BREAK UP THE HARDNESS OF HEARTS

What do Jeremiah 4:3 and Hosea 10:12 mean when discussing "fallow ground"?

THE LAST OF THE LAST DAYS

Since Jesus died and was resurrected, the world has been in the last days. With prophecies being fulfilled and the world getting darker by the minute, we are currently in the last of the last days. We need to be ready, and our conduct should be holy and godly. The lost are looking for something real. What are ways that we can present this to them?

THE COMING GREAT AND TERRIBLE DAY OF THE LORD

There is coming a day when every knee will bow, and every tongue will confess that Jesus is Lord. Those who don't accept Him as their Savior will face the terrible day of the Lord. A lost and dying world needs to hear the good news of the gospel. Take this time and ask the Lord to reveal someone you can reach out to and minister the love of Jesus to them. Please take the time to respond to whoever is laid on your heart to contact. You can do this! The Holy Spirit will be your help. Write down their name and what the Lord leads you to pray over them.

LAST DAYS CULTURE

In this last days culture, we see pressure building. The rebellious are getting more rebellious. Evil is everywhere. To stop the enemy from influencing our children, we must stand against the darkness and say, "Enough is enough!" The devil is a liar. He likes to make people believe that he is winning. We know the truth! Jesus has already won; because of that, we can win, too.

REFORMERS—THE ANTIDOTE TO A CULTURE GONE MAD

What do you think about the phrase, "Whatever the institution cannot control, it must kill or persecute"? Do you see the evidence of this thought in society today? Why or why not?

WRECKING BALL OR RECONCILER

Just as John the Baptist prepared the way for the Messiah (Jesus), we are to usher in the kingdom of God. We do this by ministering to the lost and raising young lions who will be reformers, not wrecking balls. This task requires wisdom and understanding, which can be obtained by asking the Lord to fill you with these things. Through His guidance, you can fulfill the calling on your life concerning the kingdom of God.

PUNISH THE DARKNESS

There is a spiritual warfare coming against us. What are ways that we can punish the darkness?

DIAMOND SEEDS SOWN UNDER INTENSE PRESSURE PRODUCING THE FINEST VALUE

PERSONAL REFLECTIONS

As seen in this chapter, we are at war with the enemy. He is constantly trying to destroy God's people. Many tears have been sown. God sees these tears, and He knows the battles that you are fighting. The Lord loves you more than you can even fathom. Through the hard times, He is there cheering you on and helping you through the process. If you are facing a battle, and it seems like you aren't winning, take this time to share your heart before the Lord. Ask Him to reveal a strategy that will help you through this time and win it. Because at the end of the day, the battle isn't over until you win! Write down your prayer.

CHAPTER FIVE

THE SPIRIT OF ELIJAH *ONCE AND AGAIN*

SCRIPTURES

1. Second Kings 2:9—*And so it was, when they had crossed over, that Elijah said to Elisha, "Ask! What may I do for you, before I am taken away from you?" Elisha said, "Please let a double portion of your spirit be upon me."*

2. Second Kings 2:15—*Now when the sons of the prophets who were from Jericho saw him, they said, "The spirit of Elijah rests on Elisha." And they came to meet him, and bowed to the ground before him.*

3. First Kings 19:17—*It shall be that whoever escapes the sword of Hazael, Jehu will kill; and whoever escapes the sword of Jehu, Elisha will kill.*

4. Second Kings 2:7—*And fifty men of the sons of the prophets went and stood facing them at a distance, while the two of them stood by the Jordan.*

5. Second Kings 2:3-5—*Now the sons of the prophets who were at Bethel came out to Elisha, and said to him, "Do you know that the LORD will take away your master from over you today?" And he said, "Yes, I know; keep silent!" 4 Then Elijah said to him, "Elisha, stay here, please, for the LORD has sent me on to Jericho." But he said,*

"As the LORD lives, and as your soul lives, I will not leave you!" So they came to Jericho. 5 Now the sons of the prophets who were at Jericho came to Elisha and said to him, "Do you know that the LORD will take away your master from over you today?" So he answered, "Yes, I know; keep silent!"

6. First Samuel 10:5—*After that you shall come to the hill of God where the Philistine garrison is. And it will happen, when you have come there to the city, that you will meet* ***a group of prophets*** *coming down from the high place with a stringed instrument, a tambourine, a flute, and a harp before them; and they will be prophesying.*

7. First Samuel 19:20—*Then Saul sent messengers to take David. And when they saw the group of prophets prophesying, and Samuel standing as leader over them, the Spirit of God came upon the messengers of Saul, and they also prophesied.*

8. Second Kings 4:38—*And Elisha returned to Gilgal, and there was a famine in the land. Now the sons of the prophets were sitting before him; and he said to his servant, "Put on the large pot, and boil stew for the sons of the prophets."*

9. Second Kings 6:1-2—*And the sons of the prophets said to Elisha, "See now, the place where we dwell with you is too small for us. 2 Please, let us go to the Jordan, and let every man take a beam from there, and let us make there a place where we may dwell." So he answered, "Go."*

10. Second Kings 5:22—*And he said, "All is well. My master has sent me, saying, 'Indeed, just now two young men of the sons of the prophets have come to me from the mountain of Ephraim. Please give them a talent of silver and two changes of garments.'"*

11. Second Kings 9:1—*And Elisha the prophet called one of the sons of the prophets, and said to him, "Get yourself ready, take this flask of oil in your hand, and go to Ramoth Gilead."*

12. Hebrews 11:5—*By faith Enoch was taken away so that he did not see death, "and was not found, because God had taken him"; for before he was taken he had this testimony, that he pleased God.*

13. *Matthew 11:7-15*—*As they departed, Jesus began to say to the multitudes concerning John: "What did you go out into the wilderness to see? A reed shaken by the wind? 8 But what did you go out to see? A man clothed in soft garments? Indeed, those who wear soft clothing are in kings' houses. 9 But what did you go out to see? A prophet? Yes, I say to you, and more than a prophet. 10 For this is he of whom it is written:* ***'Behold, I send My messenger before Your face, who will prepare Your way before You.'*** *11 Assuredly, I say to you, among those born of women there has not risen one greater than John the Baptist; but he who is least in the kingdom of heaven is greater than he. 12 And from the days of John the Baptist until now the kingdom of heaven suffers violence, and the violent take it by force. 13 For all the prophets and the law prophesied until John. 14 And if you are willing to receive it, he is Elijah who is to come. 15 He who has ears to hear, let him hear!"*

14. *John 1:29*—*The next day John saw Jesus coming toward him, and said, "Behold! The Lamb of God who takes away the sin of the world!"*

15. *John 3:30*—*He must increase, but I must decrease.*

16. *Matthew 17:10-13*—*And His disciples asked Him, saying, "Why then do the scribes say that Elijah must come first?" 11 Jesus answered and said to them, "Indeed, Elijah is coming first and will restore all things. 12 But I say to you that Elijah has come already, and they did not know him but did to him whatever they wished. Likewise, the Son of Man is also about to suffer at their hands." 13 Then the disciples understood that He spoke to them of John the Baptist.*

17. *Mark 9:11-13*—*And they asked Him, saying, "Why do the scribes say that Elijah must come first?" 12 Then He answered and told them, "Indeed, Elijah is coming first and restores all things. And how is it written concerning the Son of Man, that He must suffer many things and be treated with contempt? 13 But I say to you that Elijah has also come, and they did to him whatever they wished, as it is written of him."*

18. *Malachi 4:5-6*—*Behold, I will send you Elijah the prophet before the coming of the great and dreadful day of the LORD. 6And he will turn the hearts of the fathers* *to the children, and the hearts of the children to their fathers, lest I come and strike the earth with a curse.*

19. John 1:21-23—*And they asked him, "What then? Are you Elijah?" He said, "I am not." "Are you the Prophet?" And he answered, "No." 22 Then they said to him, "Who are you, that we may give an answer to those who sent us? What do you say about yourself?" 23 He said:* ***"I am 'The voice of one crying in the wilderness: "Make straight the way of the Lord,"'*** *as the prophet Isaiah said."*

20. Matthew 3:17—*And suddenly a voice came from heaven, saying, "This is My beloved Son, in whom I am well pleased."*

21. Matthew 11:2-6—*And when John had heard in prison about the works of Christ, he sent two of his disciples 3 and said to Him, "Are You the Coming One, or do we look for another?" 4 Jesus answered and said to them, "Go and tell John the things which you hear and see: 5 The blind see and the lame walk; the lepers are cleansed and the deaf hear; the dead are raised up and the poor have the gospel preached to them. 6 And blessed is he who is not offended because of Me."*

22. First Kings 19:18—*Yet I have reserved seven thousand in Israel, all whose knees have not bowed to Baal, and every mouth that has not kissed him.*

23. Luke 19:10—*For the Son of Man has come to seek and to save that which was lost.*

24. Luke 13:31-32—*On that very day some Pharisees came, saying to Him, "Get out and depart from here, for Herod wants to kill You." 32 And He said to them, "Go, tell that fox, 'Behold, I cast out demons and perform cures today and tomorrow, and the third day I shall be perfected.'"*

25. Mark 8:15—*Then He charged them, saying, "Take heed, beware of the leaven of the Pharisees and the leaven of Herod."*

26. Luke 23:8-9—*Now when Herod saw Jesus, he was exceedingly glad; for he had desired for a long time to see Him, because he had heard many things about Him, and he hoped to see some miracle done by Him. 9 Then he questioned Him with many words, but He answered him nothing.*

DEFINING THE SPIRIT OF ELIJAH

We learned that the spirit of Elijah is defined as standing against the oppression of an evil regime while operating in generational cooperation. With this understanding, have you seen or experienced the spirit of Elijah in the culture today? If so, please write about it.

GENERATIONAL EMPOWERMENT

God desires to use willing vessels on this side of heaven to accomplish His plan. Those who are reformers will not only let God use them but will also raise up those to continue to work or finish the plan once they leave earth. Think of the calling on your life. How can God use you to fulfill your calling and raise the next generation to continue or finish your God-given assignments?

DOUBLE PORTION

FOCUS POINT

According to 2 Kings 2:9, Elisha asked Elijah for a double portion of Elijah's spirit. Joseph explains that he didn't want more than what Elijah had but more than any successor would ever have. Elisha's request was a bold "ask"! Matthew 7:7 says, "Ask, and it will be given to you; seek, and you will find; knock, and it will be opened to you." Have you had times when you wanted to ask for something that was "bold" or unreachable? Notice how Elisha did, and he received it! Take this time to ask the Lord for the things you have resisted. Write down your prayer.

FIFTY WITNESSES TO ELISHA—RECEIVING THE SPIRIT OF ELIJAH

Elisha asked Elijah for a double portion, to which God gave Elisha his request and did so in front of at least fifty men. In 2 Kings 2:7, we see that these men understood what took place and bowed to the ground before Elisha out of respect. When God blesses someone, we should rejoice and celebrate with the individual. Unfortunately, jealousy and resentment often show up when God anoints and blesses someone. Why do you suppose that is? What can we do to help others see it is better to rejoice and celebrate instead?

WHO WERE THE SONS OF THE PROPHETS—WHAT WAS THE SCHOOL OF THE PROPHETS?

What was significant about "the sons of the prophets" that would differ from prophets today?

ELISHA SUCCEEDED ELIJAH

Elisha was on a mission. God revealed to him Elijah's coming translation to heaven. He also knew what would occur once Elijah was leaving; he would receive a double portion. Elisha didn't get distracted by the students who wanted to discuss the situation. Instead, he stayed focused on the mission. Have you had a word from the Lord that you knew if you spoke with others, it could distract you from the mission/word God gave you? If so, write about how you stayed focused and received what God had promised you.

ELIJAH REPRESENTS PREPARATION, REFORMATION, AND GENERATIONAL IMPARTATION!

Just like God used Elijah as a reformer, He wants to use you. Unfortunately, the devil tries to discourage people, make them feel inadequate, and fill them with shame. We need to be aware of the enemy's tactics and understand that God wants to use those who are willing and ready. Is that you? Are you ready to be used by God and to silence the enemy and all his lies? Write down a prayer of declaration.

FORERUNNER TO PART ONE AND THE UPCOMING SEQUEL!

John the Baptist was a forerunner to Jesus and carried the spirit of Elijah's anointing. This same anointing is available to the body of Christ in preparation for Jesus' return when He will take His Bride, also known as the "rapture." What steps can you take to be ready and inform others of our Lord Jesus' coming?

JOHN THE BAPTIST PREPARED AND DECLARED THE WAY OF THE LORD

John 3:30 says, "He must increase, but I must decrease." John knew it was important to become less so that Jesus could be exalted. God can use those who are humble enough to decrease so that Jesus will increase. What does this type of humility look like?

SPIRIT OF ELIJAH BEFORE THE GREAT TRIBULATION

When those around Him didn't realize who John the Baptist was, Jesus had to point out that he was Elijah, who was to come. Isn't it like God to highlight a person and their gifting and calling in front of others? When you feel like no one knows who you are, remember that God knows and is ready and actively working to let others know who you are, too!

JOHN THE BAPTIST'S RESPONSE WHEN ASKED IF HE WAS ELIJAH

John's humility is shown when asked if he was Elijah. He knew who he was and God's plan for him to "Make straight the way of the Lord." In the current season, do you know God's plan for you? If you don't, take this time to seek the Lord. Pour out your questions to Him, and then listen. He wants to speak to you and reveal things to you. Write what you hear Him saying.

LIKE ELIJAH, JOHN THE BAPTIST GOT DISCOURAGED

Elijah and John the Baptist had several things in common. One such thing is how they both felt alone and questioned either Jesus or the Lord. Even though John had heard the audible Voice of God, he still asked if Jesus was the Messiah. Jesus answered John's question by letting him know that miracles were occurring. Sometimes when we feel alone, Jesus, in His kindness, will reveal things to us that can help us in these challenging times. Have you had times when you felt this way and Jesus spoke to you in a specific way that helped you? Maybe you're in this place now. Let the Lord's kindness wash over you, and let Him speak truth to you. Write your responses and what you hear.

ELIJAH AND KING HEROD

John the Baptist had traits similar to Elijah. List some similarities between John the Baptist and Elijah.

THE SPIRIT OF ELIJAH CONFRONTS ATROCITIES AND CULTURAL EVIL

Those walking in the anointing of the spirit of Elijah will confront cultural evil. We see two different approaches between John and Jesus when coming against the spirit of Jezebel.

What were those differences, and depending on God's plan and purpose for you, how do you think you would have responded to those situations?

THE LAMB OF GOD DID NOT COME FOR POLITICAL WAR

Jesus did not come to wage war against the political figures of His time. Instead, He had a different mission, and thank God He fulfilled it! What was Jesus' mission? Why do you think God gave Jesus this mission instead of a political one?

THE LION YET TO APPEAR

Jesus and John the Baptist took different approaches toward the governments of their time. Write down their differences. Why do you think Jesus allowed a sliver of the lion to show?

A SLIVER APPEARANCE FROM THE LION

Just like the Pharisees wanted to get Jesus off His assignment, many are trying to do this to believers on God's mission. As you learn more and grow in the Lord's plan for your life, you can expect others will be more than eager to get you off task. Knowing this, how can you prepare in advance to stay strong?

JESUS CONFRONTING A FOX

In Luke 13:31-32, Jesus called Herod a "fox." Imagine Herod's response when Herod received the message. People know their sins, and they know when they are wrong. Unfortunately, many don't want others to know or call them out in sin. Jesus, in an interesting way, called out either Herod's or Herodias' sin. What do you think their response was when receiving Jesus' message?

BEWARE OF THE LEAVEN OF HEROD

In Mark 8:15, Jesus warned the disciples of the leaven of the Pharisees and Herod. He was cautioning against doctrines that were destructive and false. Sadly, many false and dangerous teachings are being taught in churches today. What are things you have either experienced or seen being taught behind pulpits that are harmful to the listeners and misleading? How should we respond?

JESUS DID MEET HEROD IN PERSON

We see that Jesus met Herod in person after Pilate sent Jesus to Herod. An interesting thing is Jesus didn't say one word to Herod. He could have but chose not to. Why do you think Jesus did this, and why is it vital to know when to speak and be silent?

ELIJAH, BEFORE THE COMING OF THE GREAT AND TERRIBLE DAY OF THE LORD

PERSONAL REFLECTIONS

We are called to be salt and light to those around us. The devil has filled so many homes, offices, and even churches worldwide. God needs us not to be timid and weak. He has equipped us with Jesus' authority to confront a culture going mad and the wisdom to know when to hold our tongues. Sometimes, war is won when we are silent in public but waging war in our prayer closet! What tends to be your typical response when confronted with evil? Have you been afraid to say things when you feel you should? Or have you said things when God has called you to be silent? How can you take what you have learned thus far and be used to the fullest of your calling in the proper way that God wants you to? Let's represent Jesus well!

CHAPTER SIX

SONS OF ISSACHAR—*MANTLED TO WATCH AND DISCERN*

SCRIPTURES

1. **First Chronicles 12:32**—*Of the sons of Issachar who had understanding of the times, to know what Israel ought to do, their chiefs were two hundred; and all their brethren were at their command.*

2. **Genesis 30:17-18**—*And God listened to Leah, and she conceived and bore Jacob a fifth son. 18 Leah said, "God has given me my wages, because I have given my maid to my husband." So she called his name Issachar.*

3. **Genesis 35:23**—*The sons of Leah were Reuben, Jacob's firstborn, and Simeon, Levi, Judah, Issachar, and Zebulun.*

4. **Genesis 49:13-14**—*Zebulun shall dwell by the haven of the sea; he shall become a haven for ships, and his border shall adjoin Sidon. 14 Issachar is a strong donkey, lying down between two burdens.*

5. **Deuteronomy 33:18-19**—*And of Zebulun he said: "Rejoice, Zebulun, in your going out, and Issachar in your tents! 19 They shall call the peoples to the mountain;*

there they shall offer sacrifices of righteousness; for they shall partake of the abundance of the seas and of treasures hidden in the sand."

6. First Chronicles 7:1-5—*The sons of Issachar were Tola, Puah, Jashub, and Shimron—four in all. 2 The sons of Tola were Uzzi, Rephaiah, Jeriel, Jahmai, Jibsam, and Shemuel, heads of their father's house. The sons of Tola were mighty men of valor in their generations; their number in the days of David was twenty-two thousand six hundred. 3 The son of Uzzi was Izrahiah, and the sons of Izrahiah were Michael, Obadiah, Joel, and Ishiah. All five of them were chief men. 4 And with them, by their generations, according to their fathers' houses, were thirty-six thousand troops ready for war; for they had many wives and sons. 5 Now their brethren among all the families of Issachar were mighty men of valor, listed by their genealogies, eighty-seven thousand in all.*

7. Ezekiel 48:25-33—*"By the border of Simeon, from the east side to the west, Issachar shall have one section; 26 by the border of Issachar, from the east side to the west, Zebulun shall have one section; 27 by the border of Zebulun, from the east side to the west, Gad shall have one section; 28 by the border of Gad, on the south side, toward the South, the border shall be from Tamar to the waters of Meribah by Kadesh, along the brook to the Great Sea. 29 This is the land which you shall divide by lot as an inheritance among the tribes of Israel, and these are their portions," says the Lord GOD. 30 "These are the exits of the city. On the north side, measuring four thousand five hundred cubits 31 (the gates of the city shall be named after the tribes of Israel), the three gates northward: one gate for Reuben, one gate for Judah, and one gate for Levi; 32 on the east side, four thousand five hundred cubits, three gates: one gate for Joseph, one gate for Benjamin, and one gate for Dan; 33 on the south side, measuring four thousand five hundred cubits, three gates: one gate for Simeon, one gate for Issachar, and one gate for Zebulun."*

8. Judges 5:15—*And the princes of Issachar were with Deborah; as Issachar, so was Barak sent into the valley under his command; among the divisions of Reuben there were great resolves of heart.*

9. Judges 10:1—*After Abimelech there arose to save Israel Tola the son of Puah, the son of Dodo, a man of Issachar; and he dwelt in Shamir in the mountains of Ephraim.*

10. *First Kings 15:27*—*Then Baasha the son of Ahijah, of the house of Issachar, conspired against him. And Baasha killed him at Gibbethon, which belonged to the Philistines, while Nadab and all Israel laid siege to Gibbethon.*

11. *Matthew 16:1-4*—*Then the Pharisees and Sadducees came, and testing Him asked that He would show them a sign from heaven. 2 He answered and said to them, "When it is evening you say, 'It will be fair weather, for the sky is red'; 3 and in the morning, 'It will be foul weather today, for the sky is red and threatening.' Hypocrites! You know how to discern the face of the sky, but you cannot discern the signs of the times. 4 A wicked and adulterous generation seeks after a sign, and no sign shall be given to it except the sign of the prophet Jonah." And He left them and departed.*

12. Galatians 5:16—*I say then: Walk in the Spirit, and you shall not fulfill the lust of the flesh.*

13. Luke 16:19-31—*There was a certain rich man who was clothed in purple and fine linen and fared sumptuously every day. 20 But there was a certain beggar named Lazarus, full of sores, who was laid at his gate, 21 desiring to be fed with the crumbs which fell from the rich man's table. Moreover the dogs came and licked his sores. 22 So it was that the beggar died, and was carried by the angels to Abraham's bosom. The rich man also died and was buried. 23 And being in torments in Hades, he lifted up his eyes and saw Abraham afar off, and Lazarus in his bosom. 24 Then he cried and said, "Father Abraham, have mercy on me, and send Lazarus that he may dip the tip of his finger in water and cool my tongue; for I am tormented in this flame." 25 But Abraham said, "Son, remember that in your lifetime you received your good things, and likewise Lazarus evil things; but now he is comforted and you are tormented. 26 And besides all this, between us and you there is a great gulf fixed, so that those who want to pass from here to you cannot, nor can those from there pass to us." 27 "Then he said, "I beg you therefore, father, that you would send him to my father's house, 28 for I have five brothers, that he may testify to them, lest they also come to this place of torment." 29Abraham said to him, "They have Moses and the prophets; let them hear them." 30 And he said, "No, father Abraham; but if one goes to them from the dead, they will repent." 31 But he said to him, "If they do not hear Moses and the prophets, neither will they be persuaded though one rise from the dead."*

14. John 20:29—*Jesus said to him, "Thomas, because you have seen Me, you have believed. Blessed are those who have not seen and yet have believed."*

15. John 4:24—*God is Spirit, and those who worship Him must worship in spirit and truth.*

16. John 20:25—*The other disciples therefore said to him, "We have seen the Lord." So he said to them, "Unless I see in His hands the prints of the nails, and put my finger into the print of the nails, and put my hand into His side, I will not believe."*

17. John 20:27—*Then He said to Thomas, "Reach your finger here, and look at My hands; and reach your hand here, and put it into My side. Do not be unbelieving, but believing."*

18. Romans 8:5-9—*For those who live according to the flesh set their minds on the things of the flesh, but those who live according to the Spirit, the things of the Spirit. 6 For to be carnally minded is death, but to be spiritually minded is life and peace. 7 Because the carnal mind is enmity against God; for it is not subject to the law of God, nor indeed can be. 8 So then, those who are in the flesh cannot please God. 9 But you are not in the flesh but in the Spirit, if indeed the Spirit of God dwells in you. Now if anyone does not have the Spirit of Christ, he is not His.*

19. Matthew 7:5—*Hypocrite! First remove the plank from your own eye, and then you will see clearly to remove the speck from your brother's eye.*

20. Galatians 6:3—*For if anyone thinks himself to be something, when he is nothing, he deceives himself.*

Why is it important to watch and discern the signs of the times today?

____

____

____

____

____

WHO WERE THESE SONS OF ISSACHAR?

In 1 Chronicles 7:1-5, we see four sons of Issachar. Incredibly, these four brothers had more than a hundred thousand sons ready for battle in their generations. These men were known as mighty men of valor! From four men came generations of mighty men and are remembered today! Being a parent, grandparent, or even a key player in a person's life has a more significant impact than one can imagine. How can you be used in this area to help develop this generation and future generations?

ISSACHAR UNDERSTOOD PUBLIC AFFAIRS

The sons of Issachar played a crucial role in public affairs. Many believers think the Church and government should be separate and not intermixed. This understanding was not present among the sons of Issachar. What has been your opinion on the subject?

IT COULD BE SAID ISSACHAR HELPED GET DAVID TO THE THRONE

The role the sons of Issachar played in bringing David to the throne is the same role that believers should play today. Many Christians decide to avoid political affairs. As the previous section stated, many think the Church and government should be separate. How can the Church get involved in political matters in a healthy and biblical way? Why is this necessary?

TWELVE ISSACHARIAN TRAITS AS THEY APPLY TO THEIR SEASON

FOCUS POINT

As we observe the many traits the sons of Issachar had, it's incredible to note that each of us has the necessary gifts and skills for our time. What are some of the things you carry that compare to the traits of the sons of Issachar? Jot them down.

THE DOOR OF REVELATORY UNDERSTANDING

Wisdom and understanding are acquired from experiences. The things we face help us grow and mature from good times to difficult times. The things we allow ourselves to see and listen to can significantly impact our understanding. With a world full of evil and pushing visual and audible travesties to bring people down, how can believers protect themselves from falling into the traps of the enemy?

TWO ORIGINS OF THE NAME ISSACHAR

We see the origin of Issachar's name. Throughout history, what someone is named has been very important. Take this time to look up the meaning of your name and write it down.

JESUS' DEFINITION OF HYPOCRITES!

Jesus used harsh wording when criticizing the religious leaders of His time. His approach could have been considered offensive and politically incorrect, but this didn't stop Jesus from saying what He said. Why did Jesus call the Pharisees and Sadducees "hypocrites"?

CARNAL AND NATURAL-MINDED PEOPLE WALK IN BLINDNESS!

Galatians 5:16 says, "I say then: Walk in the Spirit, and you shall not fulfill the lust of the flesh." What is the difference between walking in the Spirit and walking in the flesh?

THE RICH MAN AND LAZARUS

Jesus shared a parable of a rich man dying and going to hell. The rich man knew he couldn't get out but feared for his family's eternal fate if they didn't learn the truth. Unfortunately, it was too late for the rich man. Many are dying and going to hell every second of every day, and it is a sad reality and one that needs attention. The Great Commission was given to reach the lost and dying world, and we are crucial in this mission. What are ways that you are or can begin using in Jesus' commission to go into the world?

ABRAHAM'S RESPONSE

In Luke 16:19-31, why do you believe Abraham denied Lazarus' request to send someone to minister to his relatives who were still alive? Why was Father Abraham's response justifiable?

MAN LOOKS TO THE NATURAL, BUT GOD OPERATES BY FAITH

We are living in a "show me" culture, just like Thomas, who wanted to see Jesus' scars. Thomas was saying that he would only believe if he could see. Have there been times when you had a hard time believing something to be true because you didn't see it? What lesson have you learned once you were aware of John 20:29?

THERE CAN BE ONLY ONE MASTER!

Being carnal-minded can have a very detrimental effect on a believer's relationship with God. List some ways you think this to be true.

HOW TO DEVELOP DISCERNMENT

Discerning the signs of the time is very important for every believer. Many prophetic words throughout the Bible are there to prepare us for the return of Jesus for His Bride. Without discernment, hypocrisy can creep in. What are ways you can learn to discern the times?

HYPOCRITES OR ACTORS ON A STAGE

The word "hypocrite" was used to describe those who wear a mask, such as an actor. It's someone who portrays a different person when, in reality, they are the opposite of what is shown. People wear many hats, faces, and personalities depending on who they are around. How can people be more consistent with who they are versus putting on a show of someone they aren't?

HIGH-LEVEL DISCERNMENT MEANS REMOVE THE PLANK!

Why must believers examine themselves and remove the "plank" from their eyes before pointing the finger at others?

THREE MAIN THINGS THE SONS OF ISSACHAR DID

PERSONAL REFLECTIONS

Just as the sons of Issachar understood the times, knew what Israel should do, and had the proper alignment and structure to act, God has made this available to all believers. If you are in a position where you don't know the "who, what, where, when, and how," take this time to seek the Lord and ask Him to align your heart to His Word and lead you. Write what you hear Him saying.

CHAPTER SEVEN

AGENTS OF TIME—*EXTENSION, SUSPENSION, AND INTERVENTION*

SCRIPTURES

1. Isaiah 59:16—*He saw that there was no man, and wondered that there was no intercessor; therefore His own arm brought salvation for Him; and His own righteousness, it sustained Him.*

2. John 3:5-6—*Jesus answered, "Most assuredly, I say to you, unless one is born of water and the Spirit, he cannot enter the kingdom of God. 6 That which is born of the flesh is flesh, and that which is born of the Spirit is spirit."*

3. First John 4:17—*Love has been perfected among us in this: that we may have boldness in the day of judgment; because as He is, so are we in this world.*

4. Genesis 18:16-21—*Then the men rose from there and looked toward Sodom, and Abraham went with them to send them on the way. 17 And the LORD said, "Shall I hide from Abraham what I am doing, 18 since Abraham shall surely become a great and mighty nation, and all the nations of the earth shall be blessed in him? 19 For I have known him, in order that he may command his children and his household after him, that they keep the way of the LORD, to do righteousness and justice, that* *the LORD may bring to Abraham what He has spoken to him." 20 And the LORD said, "Because the outcry against Sodom and Gomorrah is great, and because their sin is very grave, 21 I will go down now and see whether they have done altogether according to the outcry against it that has come to Me; and if not, I will know."*

5. *Genesis 18:32*—*Then he said, "Let not the Lord be angry, and I will speak but once more: Suppose ten should be found there?" And He said, "I will not destroy it for the sake of ten."*

6. *Jeremiah 5:1*—*Run to and fro through the streets of Jerusalem; see now and know; and seek in her open places if you can find a man, if there is anyone who executes judgment, who seeks the truth, and I will pardon her.*

7. *Exodus 32:10-14*—*"Now therefore, let Me alone, that My wrath may burn hot against them, and I may consume them. And I will make of you a great nation." 11 Then Moses pleaded with the LORD his God, and said: "LORD, why does Your wrath burn hot against Your people whom You have brought out of the land of Egypt with great power and with a mighty hand? 12 Why should the Egyptians speak, and say, 'He brought them out to harm them, to kill them in the mountains, and to consume them from the face of the earth'? Turn from Your fierce wrath, and relent from this harm to Your people. 13 Remember Abraham, Isaac, and Israel, Your servants, to whom You swore by Your own self, and said to them, 'I will multiply your descendants as the stars of heaven; and all this land that I have spoken of I give to your descendants, and they shall inherit it forever.'" 14 So the LORD relented from the harm which He said He would do to His people.*

8. *Psalm 106:23*—*Therefore He said that He would destroy them, had not Moses His chosen one stood before Him in the breach, to turn away His wrath, lest He destroy them.*

9. *Jeremiah 15:1*—*Then the LORD said to me, "Even if Moses and Samuel stood before Me, My mind would not be favorable toward this people. Cast them out of My sight and let them go forth."*

10 . *First Corinthians 15:45-47*—*And so it is written, "**The first man Adam became a living being.**" The last Adam became a life-giving spirit. 46 However, the* *spiritual is not first, but the natural, and afterward the spiritual. 47 The first man was of the earth, made of dust; the second Man is the Lord from heaven.*

11. Joshua 10:12-14*—Then Joshua spoke to the LORD in the day when the LORD delivered up the Amorites before the children of Israel, and he said in the sight of Israel: "Sun, stand still over Gibeon; and Moon, in the Valley of Aijalon." 13 So the sun stood still, and the moon stopped, till the people had revenge upon their enemies. Is this not written in the Book of Jasher? So the sun stood still in the midst of heaven, and did not hasten to go down for about a whole day. 14 And there has been no day like that, before it or after it, that the LORD heeded the voice of a man; for the LORD fought for Israel.*

12. Isaiah 38:8*—"Behold, I will bring the shadow on the sundial, which has gone down with the sun on the sundial of Ahaz, ten degrees backward." So the sun returned ten degrees on the dial by which it had gone down.*

13. Second Kings 20:9-11*—Then Isaiah said, "This is the sign to you from the LORD, that the LORD will do the thing which He has spoken: shall the shadow go forward ten degrees or go backward ten degrees?" 10 And Hezekiah answered, "It is an easy thing for the shadow to go down ten degrees; no, but let the shadow go backward ten degrees." 11 So Isaiah the prophet cried out to the LORD, and He brought the shadow ten degrees backward, by which it had gone down on the sundial of Ahaz.*

14. Second Chronicles 32:31*—However, regarding the ambassadors of the princes of Babylon, whom they sent to him to inquire about the wonder that was done in the land, God withdrew from him, in order to test him, that He might know all that was in his heart.*

15. Exodus 33:18-23*—And he said, "Please, show me Your glory." 19 Then He said, "I will make all My goodness pass before you, and I will proclaim the name of the LORD before you. I will be gracious to whom I will be gracious, and I will have compassion on whom I will have compassion." 20 But He said, "You cannot see My face; for no man shall see Me, and live." 21 And the LORD said, "Here is a place by Me, and you shall stand on the rock. 22 So it shall be, while My glory passes by, that I will put you in the cleft of the rock, and will cover you with My hand while I pass by. 23 Then I will take away My hand, and you shall see My back; but My face shall not be seen."*

16. Genesis 1:2-3 KJV—*And the earth was without form, and void; and darkness was upon the face of the deep. And the Spirit of God moved upon the face of the waters. 3 Then God said, Let there be light: and there was light.*

17. Luke 9:30 KJV—*And, behold, there talked with him two men, which were Moses and Elias.*

18. Mark 9:4 KJV—*And there appeared unto them Elias with Moses: and they were talking with Jesus.*

19. Matthew 17:3 KJV—*And, behold, there appeared unto them Moses and Elias talking with him.*

20. Matthew 24:15-20—*"Therefore when you see the 'abomination of desolation,' spoken of by Daniel the prophet, standing in the holy place" (whoever reads, let him understand), 16 "then let those who are in Judea flee to the mountains. 17 Let him who is on the housetop not go down to take anything out of his house. 18 And let him who is in the field not go back to get his clothes. 19 But woe to those who are pregnant and to those who are nursing babies in those days! 20 And pray that your flight may not be in winter or on the Sabbath."*

21. Second Peter 3:8-12—*But, beloved, do not forget this one thing, that with the Lord one day is as a thousand years, and a thousand years as one day. 9 The Lord is not slack concerning His promise, as some count slackness, but is longsuffering toward us, not willing that any should perish but that all should come to repentance. 10 But the day of the Lord will come as a thief in the night, in which the heavens will pass away with a great noise, and the elements will melt with fervent heat; both the earth and the works that are in it will be burned up. 11 Therefore, since all these things will be dissolved, what manner of persons ought you to be in holy conduct and godliness, 12 looking for and hastening the coming of the day of God, because of which the heavens will be dissolved, being on fire, and the elements will melt with fervent heat?*

Knowing that God and the devil are territorial and humans are free moral agents, in what way can a spiritual being operate on earth?

According to John 3:5-6, Jesus said that a person is born of water and then spirit. Why is this an important understanding, and how does it show what spirits do not have?

PHYSICAL BODIED REPRESENTATIVES

How can God empower His people to actively fulfill His divine plan for the world?

HUMANS ARE THE GATEKEEPERS TO THE NATURAL WORLD

What types of events can human beings cause as free moral agents that allow access to demonic spirits?

DEFINING MOMENTS IN TIME

Just as Mount Carmel was a defining moment where God and Baal collided, is there a defining moment in your life that showed light versus darkness and light won? Write about it.

ABRAHAM ATTEMPTED TO EXTEND SODOM AND GOMORRAH'S SEASON—SUSPENDING JUDGMENT

FOCUS POINT

Similar to Abraham boldly asking the Lord to spare Sodom and Gomorrah, we are told that we can approach the throne of grace with confidence (see Hebrews 4:16). How can we stand in the gap for the lost and see the Lord work on behalf of the unsaved?

BIBLE PROPHECY CANNOT BE STOPPED, BUT CAN TIME BE ADJUSTED?

God is looking for His people to get involved. We know we can't stop what has been prophesied, but we can alter its timing. List some events that have happened where you saw the hand of God adjust its timing. Are there things you would like to see the time adjusted to a further day?

ABRAHAM MOVED THE NEEDLE IN GOD'S PLAN TO ANNIHILATE SODOM AND GOMORRAH

We see that Abraham was interceding for his nephew Lot. What is God's secret to altering the playing field and a long-planned correction event?

GOD WANTS AN INTERCESSOR!

God is looking for those who will intercede for the lost. As we have learned, God needs free moral agents to work through to fulfill His plan for the world. God has used many to fulfill His mission. List some evangelists who have said yes to God and have seen many come to know Jesus.

GOD COULD NOT FIND AN INTERCESSOR, SO, HE COUNTED ON HIMSELF

Romans 8:34 says, "It is Christ who dies, and furthermore is also risen, who is even at the right hand of God, who also makes intercession for us." Jesus is always interceding for us. Imagine that! Even if there is no one on earth standing in the gap, Jesus is and He is the ultimate intercessor and mediator. Take this time to thank Jesus for this. Write your prayer down.

SEASONS, INTERVENTION, AND SUSPENSIONS

Obedience is the key that makes reformers do the impossible. Why do you think obedience is necessary and can help weaponize a God-given revelation?

GOD DESIRES A MEDIATOR

Define what a mediator and an intercessor are. Of these two, which one do you tend to operate in? How can you grow in these gifts?

INTERRUPTIONS OF TIME

Second Peter 3:8 says, "But, beloved, do not forget this one thing, that with the Lord one day is as a thousand years, and a thousand years as one day." We see that God is outside of time. His timing is gauged way different from ours. Knowing this, in what ways do you think God could interrupt the world's realities to introduce His will?

JOSHUA SUSPENDED TIME

Joshua commanded the sun and the moon to stand still. This is an amazing example of faith and boldness. Because of this command, calendars were altered. When we are bold today, it could affect the future. How can you be bold to make a difference in the world?

ISAIAH POTENTIALLY ALTERED TIME

We know that God can do the impossible. In the situation of Isaiah, God made the shadow go backward ten degrees. This was a prophetic answer to confirm what the Lord would do. In 2 Kings 20:1, Isaiah prophesied to King Hezekiah that he would surely die. Hezekiah went on to talk to the Lord and reminded God that he had walked with God in truth and loyalty. Because of this, God heard him and responded. Have you had bad news given to you that you went to God to alter the situation? Write about it and what happened.

____

____

____

____

____

____

____

____

____

____

____

____

____

A SUNDIAL

What is the significance of the sundial in the story of Isaiah?

____

____

THE CRIES OF ISAIAH MAY HAVE CAUSED A SOLAR ECLIPSE

In whatever way God caused the shadow to move backward, we know God prolonged Hezekiah's life. God performed a miracle that is still talked about today. God knows what you need before you ask; however, He still wants you to ask. What things do you want to ask God to move but have waited because you fear it won't happen? Take this time to examine your heart to see why you feel that way. What will you do moving forward now that you have identified fear?

MOSES AND TIME TRAVEL "ACHOR" NARRATIVE

According to the word *achor,* it means *behind* and *backward.* It is exciting to think that Moses experienced the creation of the universe. How do you think Moses felt when he penned Genesis 1?

GOD IS MULTIDIMENSIONAL

Not only did God show Moses the beginning of time, He also showed Moses the future standing with Jesus on the Mount of Transfiguration. As we discussed earlier, God is not limited to time, so He can do anything He desires when working with His people. Is this understanding a new one? If so, what are your thoughts concerning this newfound information?

JESUS SHARED AN INSIGHT TO PRAYER AND THE TIMELINES OF PROPHECY

In Matthew 24:20, Jesus said we can alter the time of the "abomination of desolation." We know that the end is coming. We are living in the last of the last days. Do you tend to pray for things to be pushed back later, or are you praying for Jesus to come quickly? Neither one is a wrong prayer. Explain your stance.

IS THE TIMETABLE OF THE LORD'S RETURN MOVABLE?

PERSONAL REFLECTIONS

Second Peter 3:9 says, "The Lord is not slack concerning His promise, as some count slackness, but is longsuffering toward us, not willing that any should perish but that all should come to repentance." The Lord is patiently waiting for the lost to come home. He needs willing vessels bold enough to ask for the impossible, to push back the Lord's return so more unbelievers can turn to Him. Read Matthew 28:18-20. What did Jesus ask His disciples to do? How does this apply to all believers? What are you doing to take part in this plan?

CHAPTER EIGHT

COME UP HERE! *WATCHMAN CALL TO A GENERATION*

SCRIPTURES

1. Revelation 4:1—*After these things I looked, and behold, a door standing open in heaven. And the first voice which I heard was like a trumpet speaking with me, saying, "Come up here, and I will show you things which must take place after this."*

2. Hosea 10:12—*Sow for yourselves righteousness; reap in mercy; break up your fallow ground, for it is time to seek the Lord, till He comes and rains righteousness on you.*

3. Second Peter 3:11-12—*Therefore, since all these things will be dissolved, what manner of persons ought you to be in holy conduct and godliness, 12* ***looking for and hastening the coming of the day of God****, because of which the heavens will be dissolved, being on fire, and the elements will melt with fervent heat?*

4. Romans 12:3—*For I say, through the grace given to me, to everyone who is among you, not to think of himself more highly than he ought to think, but to think soberly, as God dealt to each one a measure of faith.*

5. *Malachi 4:5-6 KJV*—*Behold, I will send you Elijah the prophet before the coming of the great and dreadful day of the Lord: 6 and he* ***shall turn the heart of the fathers to the children,*** *and the heart of the children to their fathers, lest I come and smite the earth with a curse.*

6. *First John 4:17*—*Love has been perfected among us in this: that we may have boldness in the day of judgment; because as He is, so are we in this world.*

The Holy Spirit is summoning believers to engage with the reformation spirit of Elijah in this generation. Similar to Joseph's encounter when God called him to "Come up higher," have you had a time when the Lord spoke to you and challenged you to rise and step into the call for that season? What did He speak to you and how did you respond to His call?

____

____

____

____

____

____

____

____

____

____

____

____

____

____

WAITING ON THE LORD IS NOT A PASSIVE ACTION

Our society is in a "show me" state, and as a result, many people are waiting for God to take action. They are looking for an encounter or a supernatural experience. Why is it important that we, as individuals, shift away from this mindset and instead pursue God wholeheartedly, rather than waiting for Him to act first?

GOD IS CALLING MANY INTO ACTION SERVICE

God is always speaking. The question is, are we listening? What is vital for every believer to do when receiving an assignment from the Lord? What is the gateway to engaging the spirit of Elijah and fulfilling your role as a reformer in your generation?

SUMMONED AS A WATCHMAN ON AMERICA'S MOUNTAIN

FOCUS POINT

Throughout Scripture, we see God asking His prophets to perform prophetic acts. These require faith to step out and do what is asked without question. God asked Joseph to go to the top of Pikes Peak to symbolize his calling as a watchman to America. Has God asked you to do a prophetic act that seemed out of the ordinary? What was your response and the result?

THE PURPLE MOUNTAIN MAJESTY

Every believer has a calling in their life. No two callings are alike. Some are on the journey to be assigned over large regions, and others are called to small places. This includes workplaces, churches, neighborhoods, etc. Wherever this is, we must be ready to be used in whatever scale we are assigned. In your current season, where do you feel God has positioned you?

COME UP HIGHER BECAME CLEAR

When you hear the phrase "Come up here, come up higher," what does that mean to you? How can you apply this thought to your life?

JOHN THE REVELATOR'S HOUSE

Just as God had positioned John the Revelator as a watchman during his time, God called Joseph a "watchman to America." Describe what a watchman anointing is.

MARCHING ORDERS

The Church has a mandate to fulfill. When people receive a word from God, they have a choice. Will they shelf the word or obey the Voice of God? What is your typical response when you have received a word from the Lord?

STANDING ON NOAH'S ARK IN THE MOUNTAINS OF ARARAT

God called Noah to do an extraordinary task. It could have seemed ridiculous, especially to those who watched Noah and his sons build this massive boat. The horrors of the day, the insults and verbal abuse, and the hard labor could have been an unbearable journey. However, they stayed strong and were committed to the plan. After experiencing the raging waters and seeing humanity wiped away, imagine what Noah and his family felt when they walked off the Ark. Have you had times when you faced unprecedented challenges when trying to fulfill the word that God has given you? What helped you continue until it was fulfilled? If you are still on the journey, ask God to help you to see it to completion.

REDEMPTIVE INSTABILITY

We are facing a world similar to Noah's time, when the world was experiencing chaos and destruction. Just as God sent redemptive instability, He is in the process of doing the same thing in our age. Write a brief description of what you believe redemptive instability is.

WATCHMAN OF REDEMPTIVE INSTABILITY

In the previous question, you wrote what you believe redemptive instability is. With your answer in mind, do you see redemptive instability today? If so, explain your answer.

THE PATH OF REFORMATION

Everyone is called to walk their path of obedience to find what God has marked them for. Look up some scriptures that talk about obedience. Take this time to write down a few and meditate on them.

THE BREAKER SEED

Similar to the vision of a world made out of concrete, unsaved hearts are as hard as stone. The seed that Joseph threw symbolizes the words that he will speak, and they will be able to break up the hardened hearts. Our words have authority when backed by Jesus and His Word. Let's be willing vessels ready to speak God's Word over the hardest situations. Are you prepared to speak "breaker seeds"? If you feel the need to be better prepared, what will you do to be ready?

SPEEDING UP THE TIME

In what ways will it be evident that you are stepping into the role God has for you?

LAST DAYS ELIJAH INITIATIVE

For the spirit of Elijah to turn the hearts of the fathers back to the children and the children back to the fathers, the body of Christ must walk in alignment. What are the necessary steps for believers to walk in alignment with each other?

MOMENTS OF PREPARATION

PERSONAL REFLECTIONS

God has been preparing you to fulfill your life's call. Complicated things, travesties, joyous times, challenging people, and so on are used to help develop you into the person who will complete His call. Take this time to read Romans 5:3-5. How can you apply these verses to help you when times are tough?

CHAPTER NINE

RECONCILIATION OF FATHERS AND CHILDREN—*DESTROYING THE CURSE*

SCRIPTURES

1. First Corinthians 4:14-16—*I do not write these things to shame you, but as my beloved children I warn you. 15 For though you might have ten thousand instructors in Christ, yet you do not have many fathers; for in Christ Jesus I have begotten you through the gospel. 16 Therefore I urge you, imitate me.*

2. John 3:30—*He must increase, but I must decrease.*

3. Psalm 102:18—*This will be written for the generation to come, that a people yet to be created may praise the LORD.*

4. Proverbs 20:28-29—*Mercy and truth preserve the king, and by lovingkindness he upholds his throne. 29 The glory of young men is their strength, and the splendor of old men is their gray head.*

5. First Kings 18:21—*And Elijah came to all the people, and said, "How long will you falter between two opinions? If the Lord is God, follow Him; but if Baal, follow him."*

6. Luke 1:17—*He will also go before Him in the spirit and power of Elijah, "**to turn the hearts of the fathers to the children,**" and the disobedient to the wisdom of the just, to make ready a people prepared for the Lord.*

7. Proverbs 17:6—*Children's children are the crown of old men, and the glory of children is their father.*

8. Ephesians 4:11-13—*And He Himself gave some to be apostles, some prophets, some evangelists, and some pastors and teachers, 12 for the equipping of the saints for the work of ministry, for the edifying of the body of Christ, 13 till we all come to the unity of faith and of the knowledge of the Son of God, to a perfect man, to the measure of the stature of the fullness of Christ.*

9. Romans 16:13 NIV—*Greet Rufus, chosen in the Lord, and his mother, who has been a mother to me, too.*

10. Second Kings 2:14—*Then he took the mantle of Elijah that had fallen from him, and struck the water, and said, "Where is the LORD God of Elijah?" And when he also had struck the water, it was divided this way and that; and Elisha crossed over.*

11. First Kings 13:17-19, 23-24 NASB1995—*"For a command came to me by the word of the LORD, 'You shall eat no bread, nor drink water there; do not return by going the way which you came.'" 18 He said to him, "I also am a prophet like you, and an angel spoke to me by the word of the LORD, saying, 'Bring him back with you to your house, that he may eat bread and drink water.'" But he lied to him. 19 So he went back with him, and ate bread in his house and drank water. 23 …It came about after he had eaten bread and after he had drunk, that he saddled the donkey for him, for the prophet whom he had brought back. 24 Now when he had gone, a lion met him on the way and killed him, and his body was thrown on the road, with the donkey standing beside it; the lion also was standing beside the body.*

According to 1 Corinthians 4:14-16, there are more "instructors" than fathers. Fathers are a vital piece in the kingdom. List some reasons why you think fathers are needed.

____

____

NECESSITY OF FATHERS RATHER THAN BOY INSTRUCTORS

The phrase "ten thousand instructors" means *boy instructors*. What is the difference between a "father" and a "boy instructor"?

OPPOSITION TO GENERATIONAL RECONCILIATION

FOCUS POINT

In everything we do, we need to have the same mindset as John the Baptist, who said, "He must increase, but I must decrease" (John 3:30). What does this verse mean to you? How can we decrease so that Jesus can increase in our lives?

FATHERS AND MOTHERS STRATEGIZE FOR A GENERATION NOT YET BORN!

In today's culture, many children are raised without experiencing a father's love. Why is it important for fathers to step up in their role and pour into their children?

GENERATIONAL EXCHANGE IS THE BEGINNING OF CULTURAL ALTERATIONS

What do old and young offer each other? How can these different people groups work together?

REFORMATION COMBINES WISDOM AND STRENGTH

Proverbs 17:6 and Proverbs 20:29 each point to an aspect of generational cooperation. Why does darkness hate generational reconciliation and cooperation? What are the benefits of generational reconciliation and cooperation?

THE POWER OF SPIRITUAL FATHERS

What is the role of a spiritual father? Have you ever thought of someone as your "spiritual father" (or "mother")? If so, what about them led you to label your relationship with them as such?

FATHERS ARE THOSE YOU CAN IMITATE

Read Ephesians 4:11-13, and list the fivefold ministry offices. In what ways do these roles represent a spiritual father?

PAUL IDENTIFIED RUFUS' MOTHER AS A MOTHER FOR A TIME IN HIS LIFE

PERSONAL REFLECTIONS

The older generations are responsible for teaching the younger generations. Both generations should be in tune with the Voice of God so as not to get confused or led astray, as the young prophet believed the elder prophet over the Voice of God.

God uses fathers and mothers to direct and empower the next generation. Even if someone doesn't have kids, it does not mean they can't be a spiritual father or mother. How can you be a spiritual father or mother to those around you, even if they aren't your natural children? Every generation has someone older and wiser who can pour into them. How can you walk in submission to older and wiser people and keep God's Voice above them?

CHAPTER TEN

THE DECLINE OF INSTITUTIONS

SCRIPTURES

1. *Exodus 18:13-22*—...*Moses sat to judge the people; and the people stood before Moses from morning until evening. 14 So when Moses' father-in-law saw all that he did for the people, he said, "What is this thing that you are doing for the people? Why do you alone sit, and the people stand before you from morning until evening?" 15 And Moses said to his father-in-law, "Because the people come to me to inquire of God. 16 When they have a difficulty, they come to me, and I judge between one and another; and I make known the statutes of God and His laws." 17 So Moses' father-in-law said to him,* ***"The thing that you do is not good.*** *18 Both you and these people who are with you will surely wear yourselves out. For this thing is too much for you; you are not able to perform it by yourself. 19 Listen now to my voice; I will give you counsel, and God will be with you: Stand before God for the people, so that you may bring the difficulties to God. 20 And you shall teach them the statutes and the laws, and show them the way in which they must walk and the work they must do. 21 Moreover you shall select from all the people able men, such as fear God, men of truth, hating covetousness; and place such over them to be rulers of thousands, rulers of hundreds, rulers of fifties, and rulers of tens. 22 And let them judge the people at all times. Then it will be that every great matter they shall bring to you, but every small* *matter they themselves shall judge.* ***So it will be easier for you, for they will bear the burden with you."***

2. Joel 2:13—*So rend your heart, and not your garments; return to the LORD your God, for He is gracious and merciful, slow to anger, and of great kindness; and He relents from doing harm.*

3. Psalm 102:18—*This will be written for the generation to come, that a people yet to be created may praise the LORD.*

4. Matthew 16:25—*For whoever desires to save his life will lose it, but whoever loses his life for My sake will find it.*

5. Proverbs 24:10—*If you faint in the day of adversity, your strength is small.*

6. John 14:27—*Peace I leave with you, My peace I give to you; not as the world gives do I give to you. Let not your heart be troubled, neither let it be afraid.*

7. John 16:33—*These things I have spoken to you, that in Me you may have peace. In the world you will have tribulation; but be of good cheer, I have overcome the world.*

8. First John 4:17-20—*Love has been perfected among us in this: that we may have boldness in the day of judgment; because as He is, so are we in this world. 18 There is no fear in love; but perfect love casts out fear, because fear involves torment. But he who fears has not been made perfect in love. 19 We love Him because He first loved us. 20 If someone says, "I love God," and hates his brother, he is a liar; for he who does not love his brother whom he has seen, how can he love God whom he has not seen?*

9. First John 4:4—*You are of God, little children, and have overcome them, because He who is in you is greater than he who is in the world.*

10. Revelation 12:11—*And they overcame him by the blood of the Lamb and by the word of their testimony, and they did not love their lives to the death.*

What causes an institution to decline? Once a decline occurs, are there ways to turn it around? If so, what thoughts do you have on what can be done?

THE INSTITUTION OF THE PHARISEES

We see in Exodus 18:13-22 that Jethro gave advice to Moses that helped Moses delegate tasks and created the foundation of the Pharisees. What was the advice that Jethro gave?

What can today's leaders learn from Jethro's lesson?

JESUS COLLIDED WITH THE INSTITUTION

How did the Pharisees institutionalize Moses' revelation?

REFORMERS

FOCUS POINT

Jesus was a reformer who confronted the institutions of His time. Joel 2:13 says God is gracious, merciful, and slow to anger. Many people think God is angry, believing He will be angry at them if they mess up. Have you ever felt that way? What changed that mindset and revealed to you the true nature of God?

Take this time with the Lord and allow His Holy Spirit to minister to you.

THE FUTURE GENERATION

"This will be written for the generation to come, that a people yet to be created may praise the Lord" (Psalm 102:18). After reading that verse, why is it important that we stand up against wickedness and evil and push back against institutionalism that is set in its ways?

GIVE UP TO GO UP

What does it look like to live a life according to Matthew 16:25? How can you apply this to your life?

GENERATIONAL LEADERS

We have learned that reformers are not called to destroy an institution. What are some things they can do to keep an institution from destruction?

THE INSTITUTIONALIZED CHURCH

According to George Barna's insights, what are the four phases revealing the typical life-span of a church or ministry?

WHEN THE HORSE IS DEAD, DISMOUNT

How do we know if a ministry or organization is God-birthed versus man-birthed?

RIGHTSIZING DYING INSTITUTIONS

God desires to use reformers to bring rightsizing to institutions. What are ways you can be part of this calling?

JESUS GIVES PEACE

The world is getting darker by the minute, and tribulations and trials are coming in full force. According to John 16:33, these tribulations will worsen as the end draws near. How does Jesus encourage and offer peace?

BOLDNESS

Jesus has equipped every believer to stand against the darkness and institutions that want to choke out the Word of God. List some ways you are equipped to stand in this time.

STAND IN FAITH

PERSONAL REFLECTIONS

And they overcame him by the blood of the Lamb and by the word of their testimony, and they did not love their lives to the death.

—Revelation 12:11

Through Jesus' blood and our testimony, we can overcome anything the enemy throws our way. A testimony is something that has taken place and witnessed by someone. When we share our testimony with others, lives can be changed. A testimony can bring encouragement and strengthen people's faith. In John 9:25, the blind man responded to the Pharisees of his time by saying, "One thing I know: that though I was blind, now I see." His testimony was that he once was blind but was healed and could see! What an incredible story. If you could share a brief testimony to someone about something Jesus did, what would it be? Write it down.

CHAPTER ELEVEN

BEAST PROOF—*REFORMERS AGAINST A BABYLONIAN SYSTEM*

SCRIPTURES

1. *Matthew 16:18*—*And I also say to you that you are Peter, and on this rock I will build My church, and the gates of Hades shall not prevail against it.*

2. *Genesis 10:9*—*He was a mighty hunter before the LORD; therefore it is said, "Like Nimrod the mighty hunter before the LORD."*

3. *First Corinthians 15:45*—*And so it is written, "The first man Adam became a living being." The last Adam became a life-giving spirit.*

4. *Second Thessalonians 2:3 KJV*—*Let no man deceive you by any means: for that day shall not come, except there come a falling away first, and that man of sin be revealed, the son of perdition.*

5. *Second Kings 9:30-37*—*Now when Jehu had come to Jezreel, Jezebel heard of it; and she put paint on her eyes and adorned her head, and looked through a window. 31 Then, as Jehu entered at the gate, she said, "Is it peace, Zimri, murderer of your master?" 32 And he looked up at the window, and said, "Who is on my side? Who?" So two or three eunuchs looked out at him. 33 Then he said, "Throw her down."*

So they threw her down, and some of her blood spattered on the wall and on the horses; and he trampled her underfoot. 34 And when he had gone in, he ate and drank. Then he said, "Go now, see to this accursed woman, and bury her, for she was a king's daughter." 35 So they went to bury her, but they found no more of her than the skull and the feet and the palms of her hands. 36 Therefore they came back and told him. And he said, "This is the word of the LORD, which He spoke by His servant Elijah the Tishbite, saying, 'On the plot of ground at Jezreel dogs shall eat the flesh of Jezebel; 37 and the corpse of Jezebel shall be as refuse on the surface of the field, in the plot at Jezreel, so that they shall not say, "Here lies Jezebel."'"

6. Revelation 13:1—*Then I stood on the sand of the sea. And I saw a beast rising up out of the sea, having seven heads and ten horns, and on his horns ten crowns, and on his heads a blasphemous name.*

7. Revelation 13:16-17—*He causes all, both small and great, rich and poor, free and slave, to receive a mark on their right hand or on their foreheads, 17 and that no one may buy or sell except one who has the mark or the name of the beast, or the number of his name.*

8. Second Thessalonians 2:6-7—*And now you know what is restraining, that he may be revealed in his own time. 7 For the mystery of lawlessness is already at work; only He who now restrains will do so until He is taken out of the way.*

9. First Thessalonians 4:16-17—*For the Lord Himself will descend from heaven with a shout, with the voice of an archangel, and with the trumpet of God. And the dead in Christ will rise first. 17 Then we who are alive and remain shall be caught up together with them in the clouds to meet the Lord in the air. And thus we shall always be with the Lord.*

10. Acts 17:6 KJV—*…These that have turned the world upside down….*

11. Revelation 13:7 KJV—*And it was given unto him to make war with the saints, and to overcome them: and power was given him over all kindreds, and tongues, and nations.*

12. Revelation 2:26—*And he who overcomes, and keeps My works until the end, to him I will give power over the nations.*

13. Luke 19:13 KJV—*And he called his ten servants, and delivered them ten pounds, and said unto them,* ***Occupy till I come.***

14. Luke 19:13—*So he called ten of his servants, delivered to them ten minas, and said to them, "***Do business till I come.***"*

15. First Corinthians 3:21-23—*Therefore let no one boast in men. For all things are yours: 22 Whether Paul or Apollos or Cephas, or the world or life or death, or things present or things to come—all are yours. 23 And you are Christ's, and Christ is God's.*

16. Romans 8:28—*And we know that all things work together for good to those who love God, to those who are the called according to His purpose.*

17. Proverbs 8:22-31—*The LORD possessed me at the beginning of His way, before His works of old. 23 I have been established from everlasting, from the beginning, before there was ever an earth. 24 When there were no depths I was brought forth, when there were no fountains abounding with water. 25 Before the mountains were settled, before the hills, I was brought forth; 26 While as yet He had not made the earth or the fields, or the primal dust of the world. 27 When He prepared the heavens, I was there, when He drew a circle on the face of the deep, 28 when He established the clouds above, when He strengthened the fountains of the deep, 29 when He assigned to the sea its limit, so that the waters would not transgress His command, when He marked out the foundations of the earth, 30 then I was beside Him as a master craftsman; and* ***I was daily His delight,*** *rejoicing always before Him, 31 rejoicing in His inhabited world, and* ***my delight was with the sons of men.***

18. John 1:1—*In the beginning was the Word, and the Word was with God, and the Word was God.*

19. Romans 11:36—*For of Him and through Him and to Him are all things, to whom be glory forever. Amen.*

20. Psalm 115:16—*The heaven, even the heavens, are the LORD's; but the earth He has given to the children of men.*

21. Romans 8:19-22—*For the earnest expectation of the* ***creation eagerly waits for the revealing of the sons of God.*** *20 For the creation was subjected to futility, not* *willingly, but because of Him who subjected it in hope; 21 because the creation itself also will be delivered from the bondage of corruption into the glorious liberty of the children of God. 22 For we know that the whole* ***creation groans and labors with birth pangs*** *together until now.*

22. First John 4:4—*You are of God, little children, and have overcome them, because He who is in you is greater than he who is in the world.*

What is a Babylonian system, and what is it that this system cannot handle?

THE ANTI-ADAM

According to Josephus' words concerning Nimrod, why is it easy to speculate that Nimrod was a godless, anti-Adam leader?

THE ANTICHRIST AND THE BEAST WILL APPEAR ON THE WORLD STAGE

We are currently dealing with the spirit of Antichrist, who has not made his grand entrance. What is holding the Antichrist back from taking place in today's culture?

MACCABEES

Look up the word "revolt" in your dictionary. With the definition in mind, why do you think the Maccabees' actions were labeled the Maccabean Revolt? Do you believe that this was necessary wording for their actions? Why or why not?

WORSHIP OF ZEUS

FOCUS POINT

As Christians, we are to worship no other god except the Great God of heaven. In what ways is our current culture trying to push believers to worship other gods? How can we withstand these pressures and maintain our loyalty to the One True God?

FATHERS AND SONS SAVED JEWISH CULTURE

We see that Mattathias influenced his sons to follow in his footsteps. Fathers and mothers can pour into their children in ways others can't. If done right, children can flourish and become godly adults. If done wrong, what is the potential outcome for their future?

Kids don't get to pick their parents, but they can decide how to live once they are out of their care. How can these new adults choose to have a better outcome even if their parents weren't the best examples?

HANUKKAH

Because of the Maccabean Revolt, Israel enjoyed its independence for many years. Do you think these Maccabean knew their actions would affect Israel for many years to come? The actions of one man turned into an army ready to fight for liberty and justice. In what ways are you prepared to make a stand for something that you believe in and have a Holy Spirit conviction about?

NORMALCY BIAS

What is a basic definition of "normalcy bias," and how can believers break it off their lives?

JEZEBEL IS FALLEN

The spirit of Jezebel is present, but so is the spirit of Elijah! We don't have to be afraid. Jezebel died at the hands of her eunuchs, who listened to the voice of Jehu. The spirit of Jezebel has trapped many. Many stand confused and don't know what's right or wrong. But when the spirit of Elijah enters, clarity comes, and death to the enemy is shortly behind. After reading the story of Jezebel's death, what have you learned and can take away from this scenario?

THE BEAST

We know that in the end times, the beast will be revealed and give way to the second beast. Again, the Church is holding this off from happening. What has this understanding done for you, knowing that the Church is the restraining force holding off the Antichrist?

THE CHURCH IS BEAST PROOF

In what ways is the Church "beast proof"?

THE *EKKLESIA* CANNOT BE OVERCOME

Matthew 16:18 says, "…and the gates of Hades shall not prevail against it." The devil and hell have nothing against the Church! No matter how hard he tries, he will never prevail or win against God or the *Ekklesia*. What is the only way the devil can try to overcome or succeed in overcoming an individual on this side of heaven?

THE *EKKLESIA*

Write a brief description of the word *Ekklesia*. Do you think that every church is representing *Ekklesia*? Why or why not?

BEAST GIVEN POWER TO OVERCOME THE SAINTS

After the rapture, the Antichrist will be given power on earth to make war with those who become saints who are left on earth. In what ways do you think they will be able to hear the gospel and become believers?

TRIBULATION SAINTS

The gospel is vital today and for the time of the great tribulation. With social media preachers, televangelists, and innumerable books on salvation, people will have access to the message of the truth. How can you help prepare the salvation message that could be heard by the unsaved during the tribulation?

POWER OVER THE NATIONS

According to Revelation 2:26, how can believers gain power over the nations?

OCCUPY UNTIL I COME

We are to "occupy" until Jesus returns for His Church; what does this mean to you, and how are you "occupying" this earth as you wait for Him?

ALL THINGS ARE YOURS

When you hear the phrase "all things are yours," what does this mean to you? How can you apply this to your life and receive what God has for you?

GOD CREATED THE WORLD WITH JESUS

Jesus is the delight of the Father, and humanity is the delight of Jesus! Think about that: God delights in the Son, and the Son delights in you. How has this understanding changed the way you once perceived what God and Jesus thought about you?

AT THIS TIME, CREATION IS GROANING TO BE LIBERATED

As we eagerly await our Savior's return, creation is waiting and groaning for Jesus' return. How do you think creation is groaning and laboring with birth pangs for Jesus to come back?

TODAY YOU ARE EMPOWERED TO ACCOMPLISH THE WORKS OF GOD

PERSONAL REFLECTIONS

It has been quite the journey. You have learned what the spirit of Elijah is and how it functions today while confronting the spirits of Jezebel, Ahab, and ultimately, the Antichrist. God has equipped you to stand in this time. You are called for a purpose.

Take this final personal reflection time and examine yourself through what you have learned. How can you apply it to your life today? How can you be a father or mother to the next generation? In closing, write a prayer of dedication to the Lord as a reminder to yourself. God loves you, and so do we. God bless, and thank you for taking the time to study through this manual.

ABOUT THE AUTHOR

Joseph Z is an international prophetic voice who builds lives by the Word of God in the Church, government, and marketplace.

He founded the nonprofit organization Z Ministries, a parent entity for multiple conferences, specialized ministries, and social media events.

Joseph broadcasts *live* each weekday morning for one hour of teaching and prophetic ministry on the Joseph Z Facebook page and through JosephZ.com.

Joseph and his wife, Heather, have two amazing children, Alison and Daniel, and reside in the beautiful state of Colorado, USA.

In the Right Hands, This Book Will Change Lives!

Most of the people who need this message will not be looking for this book. To change their lives, you need to **put a copy of this book in their hands.**

Our ministry is constantly seeking methods to find the people who need this anointed message to change their lives. **Will you help us reach these people?**

Extend this ministry by sowing three, five, ten, or *even more* books today and change people's lives for the better! Your generosity will be part of catalyzing the Great Awakening that many have been prophesying and praying for.

FOR FURTHER INFORMATION

If you would like prayer or further information about Joseph Z Ministries, please call our offices at

(719) 257-8050 or visit **JosephZ.com/contact**

Visit JosephZ.com for additional materials.

Joseph and Heather have ministered together for over 20 years; with a passion to see others be all they are called to be. For many years, Joseph & Heather have had the heart to offer life-changing materials and teaching at no cost to the body of Christ. Today, they have made that a reality by offering various media resources and biblical training free of charge. Joseph and Heather currently reside in Colorado Springs, CO with their two children, Alison and Daniel.

Learn more at
www.josephz.com

From

JOSEPH Z

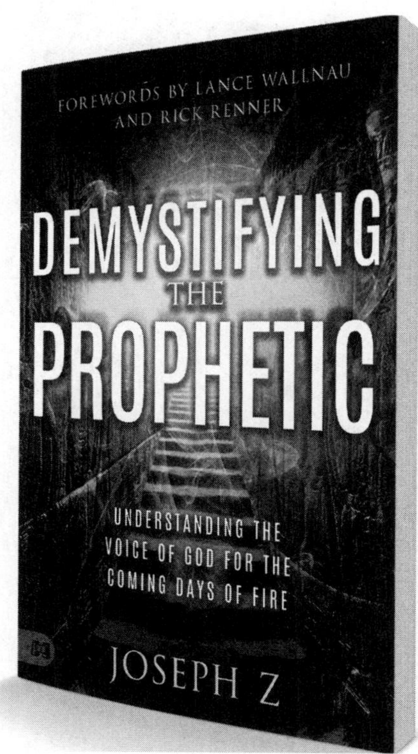

Navigate the End Times With Prophetic Precision

Never before have we had a greater need for clear, prophetic insight. Our world is teeming with widespread prophetic error, controversy, and deception—discrediting the legitimate prophetic voices God is using to speak to us. We need true biblical prophecy to take its place at the forefront of our lives.

Joseph Z, internationally respected prophetic voice, began encountering the Voice of God from a young age through dreams and visions. With wisdom, accuracy, biblical balance, and experience, Joseph offers powerful keys to help you unlock the revelation, interpretation, and application of prophecy.

The stakes have never been higher. Only true and refined prophecy cuts through the deception with unmatched power and precision. Both the Church and the world are in desperate need for this elevated prophetic encounter. Now, Jesus urgently seeks to equip you to navigate these critical last days with prophetic insight.

Purchase your copy wherever books are sold

From

JOSEPH Z

Your Next Move Will Unleash Heaven's Power

A cosmic war rages around us, and the forces of darkness are tightening their grip on humanity. Are you overwhelmed by relentless spiritual attacks, sensing the weight of unseen forces crushing your spirit?

You weren't born to be a victim—you were created to annihilate the enemy!

Since the fall of Lucifer, the heavens have been locked in a savage battle between the armies of light and the demonic hordes of hell. Now, these ancient powers are targeting this generation, and the Church stands at the epicenter of this apocalyptic clash. The question is: Will you rise to the fight or be consumed?

The demonic hosts tremble when a believer steps into their true authority, and now is your moment to become a weapon in the hands of the Almighty.

The war has already begun, but the victory is yours for the taking. Your next move will unleash the fury of heaven and decimate the powers of darkness. The question is: Are you ready?

Purchase your copy wherever books are sold